The Internet
for the
Older Generation

Other Books of Interest

Acknowledgements

The author and publishers would like to thank the following for their help in the preparation of this book:

James Foster (Internet Marketing Manager) of HBOS plc for kindly providing Halifax plc and Bank of Scotland information.

Paul Johnson, Image Library Manager, The National Archives, Kew (formerly the Public Record Office) for permission to reproduce extracts from the 1901 Census Online.

Michael Dibben, The Tarbert Hotel, Penzance, Cornwall.

Mark Gatenby, The Gatenbys of Yorkshire Web Site.

The Internet
for the
Older Generation

Jim Gatenby

BERNARD BABANI (publishing) LTD
The Grampians
Shepherds Bush Road
London W6 7NF
England

www.babanibooks.com

Please Note

Although every care has been taken with the production of this book to ensure that any projects, designs, modifications and/or programs, etc., contained herewith, operate in a correct and safe manner and also that any components specified are normally available in Great Britain, the Publishers and Author do not accept responsibility in any way for the failure (including fault in design) of any project, design, modification or program to work correctly or to cause damage to any equipment that it may be connected to or used in conjunction with, or in respect of any other damage or injury that may be so caused, nor do the Publishers accept responsibility in any way for the failure to obtain specified components.

Notice is also given that if equipment that is still under warranty is modified in any way or used or connected with home-built equipment then that warranty may be void.

© 2003 BERNARD BABANI (publishing) LTD

First Published - May 2003
Reprinted - July 2003
Reprinted - December 2003
Reprinted - February 2004
Reprinted - May 2004

British Library Cataloguing in Publication Data:

A catalogue record for this book is available from the
British Library

ISBN 0 85934 600 5
Cover Design by Gregor Arthur
Printed and bound in Great Britain by Cox and Wyman Ltd

About this Book

This book attempts to show, in plain English, that older people have much to gain by using the Internet. The first chapter outlines some of the many ways the Internet can help with daily life, from home shopping to keeping in touch with friends and family around the world. It also dispels the myth that computers are difficult to use, since modern computers are controlled by the simple click of a mouse button. The next chapter gives advice on setting up an "Internet-ready" computer in your home and explains the technical jargon used by the computer trade, which alienates so many people.

A chapter is devoted to Microsoft Windows, which controls everything you do with your computer. There is also a description of the help, built into Microsoft Windows, for users with impaired mobility, hearing and eyesight.

The process of connecting to the Internet is described, with advice on choosing an Internet Service Provider and discussion of the latest high speed *broadband* services. Using a "browser" program to search for and display Web pages is explained, together with Internet activities such as home banking, finding a holiday and tracing family history.

Many older people wish to keep in touch with friends and relatives in this country and abroad. This is discussed at length in the chapters on e-mail, including the sending of photographs as e-mail "attachments".

The preparation of photographs using a digital camera and a scanner is also covered, followed by a description of the posting of photos onto a Web site, viewable anywhere in the world by anyone with an Internet connection. Creating your own simple Web site is also described in some detail.

About the Author

Jim Gatenby trained as a Chartered Mechanical Engineer and initially worked at Rolls-Royce Ltd using computers in the analysis of performance. He obtained a Master of Philosophy degree in Mathematical Education by research at Loughborough University of Technology and taught mathematics and computing to 'A' Level for many years. His most recent posts included Head of Computer Studies and Information Technology Coordinator. During this time he has written many books in the fields of educational computing and Microsoft Windows.

The author has considerable experience of teaching students of all ages and abilities, in school and in adult education. For several years he successfully taught the well-established CLAIT course and also GCSE Computing and Information Technology.

Trademarks

Microsoft, MSN, Outlook Express, FrontPage, Hotmail, Windows, and Windows XP are either trademarks or registered trademarks of Microsoft Corporation. AOL is a trademark of America Online, Inc. Netscape and Netscape Navigator are trademarks of Netscape Communications Corporation. Norton AntiVirus is a trademark of Symantec Corporation. nero-BURNING ROM is a trademark of Ahead Software AG. Easy CD Creator is a trademark or registered trademark of Roxio Inc. Paint Shop Pro is a trademark or registered trademark of JASC Inc. Adobe Photoshop is a trademark of Adobe Systems Incorporated.

All other brand and product names used in this book are recognized as trademarks or registered trademarks, of their respective companies.

Contents

4

Help for Users With Special Needs   **43**

5

Internet Service Providers   **53**

8

9

10

11

12

13

More About Modems

Why Use
The Internet?

Introduction

This chapter aims to show that there is a great deal for older people to gain from using computers and the Internet. We often see the amazing computing exploits of young children on television and in the media and this can give the impression that computers are only for the young. Some older people feel unable to cope with computing because they think it is too difficult. As an experienced teacher of all ages from eleven to eighty I know this is not true.

Of course there are many children who show great aptitude in the use of computers, particularly in playing games. Most children nowadays start to use computers at primary school, while many older people have missed out altogether, through no fault of their own.

Arthur is 71 years old. In a typical week he might:

- Build some new computers for people in his village.
- Carry out some computer repairs and upgrades.
- Demonstrate Broadband to a friend.
- Obtain some music free from the Internet.
- Make a CD for his grandson, containing free games copied from the Internet.

Of course, not all older people want to get involved in the technical side of computing like Arthur. However, older people certainly have the ability to make good use of computers and the Internet to enrich their lives in many different ways. In later life there is usually more time to learn new skills at a leisurely pace, without the pressures of holding down a full-time job or looking after a family.

Anyone Can Use a Modern Computer

Tremendous efforts have been made in recent years to make computers easy to use. There is no longer any need to learn complicated commands or technical jargon. If you were put off computing years ago because it was so complex, you can forget your past experience and make a fresh start. Nowadays nearly everything can be done by

 moving a small device known as a "mouse", then pressing a button to select an object or instruction from the screen. It's as easy as navigating the teletext on TV.

Moving the mouse about the desk causes a small *pointer* (shown right and below) to move across the screen. To select a task or object on the screen, the pointer is moved over the task and a button (usually the left-hand one) is pressed on the mouse.

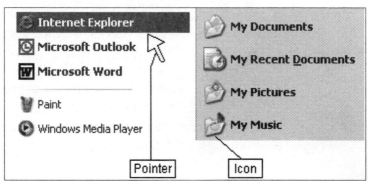

Help for People with Special Needs

If you're worried about physical impairments such as failing eyesight or mobility, the latest computer systems have built-in help, known as *Accessibility* features. These include a *magnifier* to display an enlargement of the text on the screen. There is also an *on-screen keyboard* operated by the mouse, for anyone who finds a conventional keyboard difficult to use.

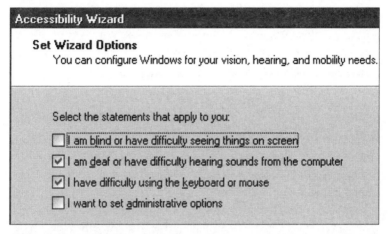

Help for users with special needs is covered in more detail later in this book.

The Arrival of the Internet

The greatest phenomenon in the last few years has been the explosion of the Internet. No business or organization worth its salt is without a "Web site". This is usually several pages of information (both text and pictures) about the organization. These Web pages are posted up on special computers all over the world, known as *Web servers*. Anyone with a computer connected to the Internet can view these Web pages from anywhere in the world.

Business Web sites often allow orders to be placed "on-line" via the Internet. Many small businesses have benefited from the Internet. A recent report announced that 83% of the farms in Britain are now connected to the Internet, enabling them to advertise their farm produce and to promote other activities such as bed and breakfast accommodation.

What Use Is the Internet?

The Internet is not just a tool to promote business. In fact, anyone and everyone can benefit across a wide range of on-line activities, as outlined in the following pages.

Obtaining Information on Any Subject

School children have been using the Internet to research homework topics for some years. However, older people can also benefit from this enormous store of knowledge. You can find out about any subject, such as health, holidays, gardening, sport and news. The information is up-to-date and usually prepared by experts in a particular field. There is much information on medical conditions, compiled by doctors and also including contributions from patients. Unlike the traditional encyclopedia in book form, information can be kept completely up-to-date.

Education On-line

You can learn new subjects on-line under schemes such as Learndirect. Anyone can obtain educational materials by "downloading" them to their own computer.

Downloading involves copying *files* such as text, graphics, photographs, music, video or software from the Internet, then saving it on your own computer. The term *file* refers to any sort of information, text, graphics, music, etc., saved on a computer disc.

Keeping In Touch With Friends and Family

You can communicate with contacts around the world using e-mail. An e-mail consists of a letter or message typed at the keyboard. The e-mail can also include *attachments* such as photographs or video clips. Depending on the person receiving the e-mail (and how often they check their electronic "mailbox"), e-mail can be almost instantaneous anywhere in the world.

Researching Your Family History

Huge databases on the Internet such as the 1901 Census allow us to trace our ancestors and build up a family tree.

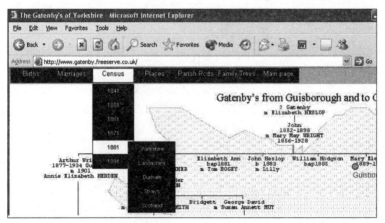

Some Web sites allow you to post up notices asking for information about long-lost relatives. These can be seen by millions of people anywhere the world and often lead to rewarding contacts. This can start a dialogue carried out across the world by e-mail and may result in reunions of friends and families. There are also many Web sites listing parish records and giving advice and help in compiling family trees. This subject is covered in more detail later in this book.

Internet Shopping

On-line shopping allows you to browse catalogues and purchase books, groceries, music, etc., from the comfort of your own home. Major supermarkets such as Tesco and Sainsbury have built up significant on-line shopping enterprises, saving the time and effort of the conventional weekly shopping trip.

After completing your initial order on-line, the system "remembers" your shopping list and this can be used as the basis for your future weekly shopping. In subsequent weeks you only have to select any new items and confirm or omit the items on your basic list. On-line shopping can literally reduce an entire week's shopping to just a few minutes at the computer.

Holiday Accommodation

Many hotels and other providers of holidays allow you to view the accommodation and check vacancies on your screen before making a reservation on-line.

Unlike the conventional holiday brochure, the information on the Web site should be absolutely up-to-date and there is instant communication on-line for bookings and further information. Once connected to the Internet, you can *immediately* find holiday information for destinations anywhere in the world - you don't have to wait while brochures are sent to you by the traditional post.

Internet Banking

Internet Bank accounts can be opened, usually offering a higher rate of interest than conventional accounts in High Street branches. Funds can be transferred on-line between various accounts.

Obtaining Music and Software

Freely available copies of music, video clips and computer software can be downloaded, i.e. transferred from the Internet and saved on your own computer.

Although other members of my family never spend more than an hour or so a week on the Internet, the next page lists a few of the things we did in the last few months. Many of the tasks could not have been done at all without the Internet. All of the tasks would have taken longer by traditional methods.

One Family's Use of the Internet

- Booked holidays after checking daily vacancies, pictures and descriptions of the accommodation.

- Found up-to-date, high quality information about a serious illness.

- Carried out weekly supermarket shopping in about 15 minutes, delivered to the door.

- Traced and renewed contact with a cousin in England, not heard of for nearly 40 years.

- Located unheard-of relatives in Canada. Received messages and family photographs by e-mail.

- Printed out a family tree, otherwise unavailable.

- Used the 1901 On-line Census to find details of relatives alive at that time, including addresses, occupations and household members.

- Ordered books and music, delivered the next day.

- Obtained special detailed weather forecasts and flight information for pilots.

- Traced the source of the River Dove in the Staffordshire Moorlands.

- Received examination results at midnight, almost 36 hours before the paper copy arrived in the post.

- "Downloaded" software and music from the Internet straight to our computer.

- Found information about plants, shrubs and gardening equipment.

- Opened an Internet bank account offering an above-average interest rate. Transferred funds on-line.

Summary - Why Use the Internet?

The purpose of this chapter was to show you that older people have much to gain by using computers and the Internet. No-one need worry about the supposed difficulty of learning new computing skills; modern systems have been designed and tested to make sure they are easy for normal people to use. Most tasks just require you to "point and click" at simple instructions and menus on the screen.

If you find physical tasks difficult for any reason, there are various *accessibility features* built into the latest computer systems. These features are intended to help people with common impairments and are described in Chapter 4.

Forget the popular image of the Internet as a plaything for young "whiz kids" trying to "hack" into banks and military installations or spread deadly computer viruses. As listed earlier in this chapter and described in more detail later in this book, there is a multitude of worthwhile, sensible uses of the Internet, from which older people can benefit. With the extra time often available in later life, the Internet can become a mentally stimulating and rewarding hobby. Also, as many older people (including myself) have found, computing and the Internet can be the starting point for an interesting new career or small business.

After reading this book (and perhaps the companion volume "Computers for the Older Generation" from Bernard Babani (publishing) Ltd), you may wish to join one of the many computing courses. The popular CLAIT scheme covers most aspects of computer use including the Internet. These courses are held at local adult education centres, often with a choice of either daytime or evening sessions. Such courses are usually very friendly and supportive, allowing you to progress at your own rate.

Getting Set Up

Choosing a Location

Once you have decided to become an Internet user, you can start planning your set-up. An important consideration is to find a suitable location in your home. If you are fortunate enough, the ideal solution is a small room which you can turn into a dedicated computer room, with few distractions. This will give you the space to set up your computer on its own desk or table, with enough room for the essential handbooks and accessories such as CDs and floppy discs.

Safety and Security

Computers are very popular with thieves, so try to make sure your computer is not clearly visible from outside. If you choose to base your computer in a shed or other outbuilding, make sure it is secure and not damp.

A modern computer system including all of the peripheral devices such as a printer and a scanner can easily require six or more power points. For safety reasons you should not overload your power points or have a "bird's nest" of wires trailing all over the floor. It may be advisable to have some extra power points professionally installed. Faulty wiring might invalidate insurance policies in the event of a fire.

Connecting to a Telephone Line

Your computer will need to be connected to a telephone socket in order to access the Internet and send and receive e-mails and information from Web sites. Depending on the type of Internet connection you choose, this may mean that you will not be able to use the telephone at the same time as the Internet. This subject is discussed in more detail later, but a brief explanation follows.

The 56K Modem

Traditionally computers have been connected to the telephone lines by a device called a *modem*. In recent years this has been known as the *56K modem*, the term "56K" referring to the speed at which data is transmitted.

1 K or Kilobit means 1024 bits. It takes 8 bits to represent a letter of the alphabet or a number in the range 0-9.

A 56K modem is therefore *nominally* capable of sending and receiving data at roughly 56,000 bits per second. In practice much lower speeds (such as 33,000 bits per second) are achieved when sending data to the Internet.

The 56K modem connects into the telephone line through an adapter with two sockets. A cable from the computer via the modem connects into one socket, while the ordinary telephone handset is plugged into the other socket. When you are on-line to the Internet through a 56K modem, you can't use the telephone at the same time.

Separate Telephone Line

This problem can be solved, at a price, by having a second telephone line installed and dedicating it to the Internet. With a separate telephone line for the Internet you can be billed separately for your Internet telephone charges, as distinct from your normal household telephone bill. This would be helpful if your Internet connection is used for business and you can set your Internet telephone charges against profits, for tax purposes.

Broadband Connection

The latest method of connecting to the Internet is called *broadband* and works very much faster than the 56K modem.

The broadband system allows the Internet and the telephone to be used at the same time.

To save unnecessary expense, it would be prudent to choose between the traditional modem and the broadband system *before* buying your computer and this choice is discussed in more detail shortly. (At the time of writing, some telephone exchanges in Britain are not ready to deliver broadband; this can be checked with BT).

If you live in an area where the pavements have been dug up to lay cables for cable television, then you can also consider connecting to the Internet by a *cable modem*.

Choosing a Computer System

Most computers sold in the High St. are known as *PCs*, after the original IBM Personal Computer. In fact there are thousands of manufacturers and assemblers building PCs. Most of these machines use the Microsoft Windows operating system, which controls the screen display and the overall operation of the computer. This is achieved through a system of windows and icons on the screen, selected by a mouse.

The PC has become the world-wide standard for home and business computers and has generated a huge amount of software. There is also plenty of support for the PC, including spare parts and people experienced in carrying out repairs and upgrades to keep the machines up-to-date.

Nowadays the only serious alternative to the PC computer is the Apple Macintosh, in various forms. The Apple Mac has many devoted users since it was the pioneer of easy-to-use mouse and windows operating systems. The Mac has established itself as the preferred choice in many printing and publishing enterprises and in areas of education.

For the general user, however, who wishes to remain in the mainstream of readily-available software, hardware and support, there is really no choice other than to buy a PC machine running Microsoft Windows.

Choosing a Supplier

When buying a computer system, you may choose to visit one of the large retailers who often put together some very attractive packages, often including a printer, 56K modem and a document scanner. Such a system might be purchased for around £800 including VAT.

Alternatively you might purchase a computer from one of the many small independent companies who build their own computers for as little as £500 including VAT. These are usually one or two person enterprises and they will often build a computer to the customer's own specification. For example, you might wish to include a faster *processor*, or more *memory* or a bigger *hard disc drive* than standard. (These terms are explained in the next few pages).

If possible, try to find a business that has been around for a few years and is recommended by genuine satisfied customers. The advantage of this sort of supplier is that you can go back to the person who has built your computer should there be any problems. In the case of the large supplier or mail order company, your computer may need to be sent away for repair and may not be seen again for several weeks. In the large company your point of contact may be a sales person with little or no technical expertise. Fortunately modern computers are very reliable if used sensibly and you will probably have very few problems.

Plan for the Future

If you buy one of the current computer systems it will almost certainly be powerful enough to cope with using the Internet. However, it's worth bearing in mind that computers quickly become out of date as software companies design ever more demanding programs. Therefore it's a good idea to buy the most powerful computer your budget will allow. The power of a computer is determined by components such as the processor, the memory and the hard disc drive and these terms are explained in the next few pages.

The Computer Specification

Shown below is the specification of a typical computer from one of the large suppliers. Many of these terms may look like meaningless jargon, so they are explained in more detail in the next few pages.

- **Intel Pentium 4   2.53GHz Processor**
- **DVD and CD-Rewriter Drives**
- **512MB RAM**
- **80GB Hard Drive**
- **64MB GeForce Graphics**
- **Stereo Sound and Speakers**
- **Microsoft Windows XP**
- **Microsoft Works 7.0**
- **56K Modem**
- **17-inch monitor**
- **Price £799 including VAT.**

A computer to the above specification will be more than adequate for using the Internet. In fact, any of the computers sold in the last few years should suffice for general use of the Internet, i.e. searching for information and sending and receiving e-mails. Let's now try to decipher the jargon in the above specification and understand what each of the terms means, in plain English.

The Jargon Explained

The Processor

This is the "brains" of the computer. It is the micro-chip which carries out all of the high speed instructions and calculations. The Intel Pentium is the most well-known brand of processor, but there are rivals such as the AMD Athlon and Duron processors. "2.53GHz" in the previous specification refers to the speed the processor carries out instructions. I am still using a 1GHz machine which is quite adequate for general Internet use, so the 2.53GHz should have a good degree of built-in "future proofing".

MHz or megahertz is a measure of the speed of the processor in millions of instructions per second.

1GHz or gigahertz is roughly 1000 megahertz.

DVD and CD-Rewriter Drives

These are devices which allow you to copy music, video and data files onto blank CDs. So you can download music from the Internet and copy it onto a blank CD for use in an ordinary CD player. The DVD re-writer allows you to make copies of video files onto a DVD disc, which looks similar to an ordinary CD.

The RAM

RAM stands for *Random Access Memory*. It is a *temporary store* in the computer and holds the programs and data currently being used. 512MB is a measure of the storage capacity of the RAM. 512MB is quite generous by today's standards, 256MB being common on many new computers.

1MB or megabyte is the memory needed to store about 1 million characters such as letters of the alphabet or the numbers 0-9.

The Hard Drive

When you switch the computer off the data stored in the RAM (also called simply the *memory*) is lost.

So you need a permanent storage device to keep your programs and work files (such as word processing documents). The hard drive consists of a set of magnetic discs on which you can record or *save* all of the software and also all of the data files which you produce. This will also include your e-mails and any Web pages and files downloaded from the Internet.

80GB in the previous specification is a good size hard disc - many new machines are supplied with "only" 40GB. This may be adequate for many purposes and is itself phenomenal compared with hard disc drives of a few years ago. As can be seen from the screenshot below, my current machine has a relatively puny 19GB hard disc, of which 14.5GB are still unused.

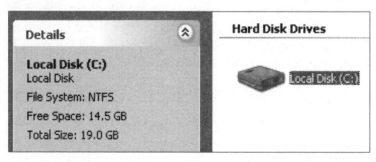

However, if you intend to store a lot of photographs or large games, make sure you buy the biggest hard disc you can afford.

A GB or gigabyte is approximately 1000 MB.

The Graphics Card

This is a set of microchips plugged into the computer on what is known as an *expansion board*. The graphics card controls the quality of the screen display. For general use the standard graphics card supplied with most computers should suffice. However, anyone doing a lot of high precision drawing or graphics work or playing high resolution games or using simulations may want to specify a high quality graphics card, such as the GeForce model listed on the previous specification.

Microsoft Windows XP

The Microsoft Windows operating system is dominant on personal computers throughout the world. The Windows system enables you to "drive" the computer using a mouse and a series of on-screen menus and icons which represent different tasks and programs. The screen is divided up into one or more "windows" or frames. Shown below is a screen showing two windows; the window on the right containing this page as it is typed in the word processor. The window on the left contains a feature called the **Control Panel**, which is used for setting up hardware and software.

Windows XP contains a lot of extra built-in software. This includes Internet Explorer, a *Web browser* or program which allows you to find and display pages on the Internet.

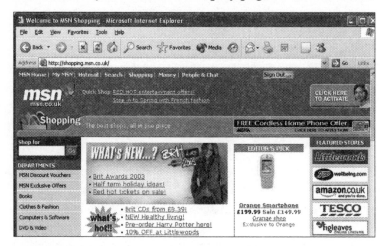

As you can see above, a Web page can contain a lot of advertisements which help to finance the service. Most Web pages also contain several *links* or *clickable* icons or text. Clicking on a link opens up another Web page.

Microsoft Windows, Internet Explorer and Web pages are discussed in more detail in the next few chapters.

Microsoft Works

This is a "suite" of several programs often included free with a new computer system. It can also be bought separately, often for less than £100. Microsoft Works includes all of the software needed to do the basic office tasks of *word processing* (typing documents and reports), *spreadsheets* (calculations on tables of figures and accounts) and *database* (creating files of records which can be searched and sorted).

The 56K Modem

This is a small device for connecting a computer to the telephone line so that data can be sent (*uploaded*) and received (*downloaded*).

At the time of writing the 56K modem is being challenged by the much faster but more expensive broadband system, discussed in detail shortly. Many new computers are supplied with a 56K modem fitted as standard. It's a simple job to fit a modem if your computer doesn't have one.

The Monitor

This is the screen on which you view your programs or Web pages. A 17-inch monitor has an actual viewing size of somewhat less, perhaps 15.7 inches or so. If you are short of desk space and your budget allows, you may wish to consider one of the more expensive flat TFT (*Thin-Film Transistor*) screens.

The Printer

Although not included in the previous specification, a printer is essential to make full use of a computer. A printer is necessary for all of the documents you intend to create and to make copies of Web pages and any messages and photographs you receive with e-mails. You may also wish to obtain a digital camera so that you can use the computer to edit and print your own photographs.

The inkjet printer is now the most popular for general home and small office use. They are cheap to buy and allow high quality printing in black and white and colour. Some excellent results can be obtained with photographs, especially if special photographic paper is used.

The main drawback is that while inkjet printers can be obtained for about £40 upwards, the cost of *genuine* black and colour ink cartridges (typically £20-£30) can soon eclipse the cost of buying the printer. Compatible cartridges from third-party suppliers generally cost a fraction of the price of the genuine article.

Shown below is a photograph of the popular Epson Stylus C60 inkjet printer.

For very large quantities of black and white printing a *laser printer* may be more suitable. These can cost anything from £100 up to several hundred pounds for an office standard machine capable of heavy use all day and every day.

Installing the New Computer

Once you have purchased your system, your supplier may be prepared to install the system in your home and make sure everything is working. If you have to set up the system yourself, take comfort from the fact that it's virtually impossible to fit any of the cables incorrectly.

This subject is discussed in more detail in the companion volume to this book, "Computing for the Older Generation" from Bernard Babani (publishing) Ltd.

Suggested Questions for Computer Suppliers

So that you won't be "blinded with science" at the computer shop, do some preparation for your visit. You might prepare a list of questions - a good supplier will have no problem in giving you honest answers. A few ideas are given below.

- What system would best suit your intended use of the computer?
- Is it easy to upgrade the computer in the future, with more memory, faster processor, bigger hard disc, more expansion cards?
- What guarantee is included with the machine and what does it cover?
- What are the arrangements for returning the machine and who pays for transportation?
- What is a typical turnaround time for repairs?
- What software is pre-installed on the machine - Windows, word processor, spreadsheet, etc.?
- What peripherals are included - printer, scanner, digital camera, etc.?
- Would the basic machine without these "free" peripherals be better value? Also, you may want a better printer, for example, than the one included in the package.
- Will the supplier deliver the computer and get it up and running in your home?
- Would they give you any free tuition to get you started?

After buying a new machine, keep all receipts and packaging in case the system has to be returned for repair.

Broadband Connections

Some people find the traditional 56K modem too slow, particularly if they send or receive very large files across the Internet. These files might include software, music, videos, or photographs for example. One answer to the need for more speed is the new broadband system, introduced by BT and others. Home users of broadband have a service known as ADSL (Asymmetric Digital Subscriber Line). This converts a standard telephone line into a very fast Internet line. Comparing broadband to a normal modem line is like comparing a 6-lane motorway to a narrow country lane.

At the time of writing broadband is starting to take off, after a slow start in Britain. Some rural areas of Britain still can't access broadband because their telephone exchanges need modification. BT will not modify a telephone exchange unless a certain number of subscribers register for the service.

Even if your local telephone exchange is delivering broadband, you should check with BT that your home can receive broadband. They will check out the cable to your home and, if necessary, set up the actual connection. Alternatively you can set up broadband yourself from a kit provided by BT or another provider; this includes an ADSL modem, one or more small connecting devices known as *filters* and a CD containing the essential software..

To obtain a broadband connection, you will need to subscribe to a broadband Internet Service Provider such as BT Broadband or AOL. Alternatively, if your road has been dug up to install the cables for cable television, there is a Cable Broadband service available from companies such as NTL. This requires a special *cable modem.*

If you are already connected to the Internet with an
ordinary modem and want to know more about broadband,
the BT Web site (**http://www.bt.com/**) has details of prices
and equipment needed, as shown below.

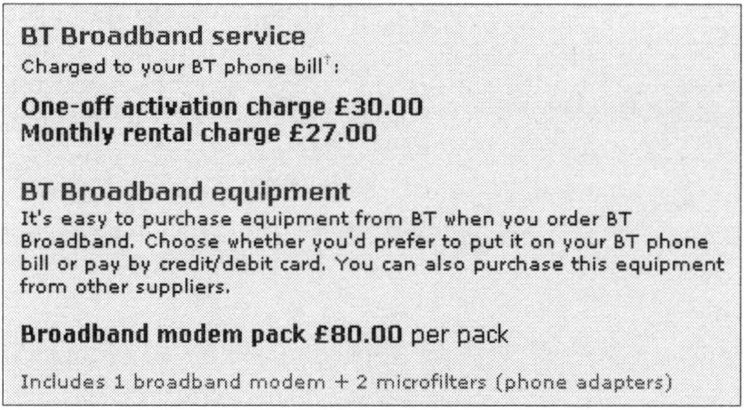

BT Broadband service
Charged to your BT phone bill[1]:

One-off activation charge £30.00
Monthly rental charge £27.00

BT Broadband equipment
It's easy to purchase equipment from BT when you order BT
Broadband. Choose whether you'd prefer to put it on your BT phone
bill or pay by credit/debit card. You can also purchase this equipment
from other suppliers.

Broadband modem pack £80.00 per pack

Includes 1 broadband modem + 2 microfilters (phone adapters)

You can also enter your telephone number and find out if
your local telephone exchange can deliver Broadband.

Can I get
BT Broadband?
Enter telephone number:

Check »

BT Broadband gives you a fast Internet connection which
you can use with an Internet Service Provider of your
choice such as AOL. BT Openworld Broadband is BT's
own Internet Service, providing content such as music and
sport, as well as e-mail addresses and space for Web pages
you have created.

Broadband Features

Below is a list of the main features of a broadband Internet connection:

- Broadband is up to 10 times faster than an ordinary 56K modem, making it possible to view film clips and music videos.

- You can send e-mails including pictures and video in *seconds* rather than *minutes*.

- You can download large files such as software, pictures and graphics from the Internet, in a fraction of the time taken by a 56K modem. These are then saved on the hard disc of your computer.

- Once up and running, the computer is *always connected to the Internet*.

- A monthly fee of about £20-£30 usually includes unlimited access to the Internet. There are no call charges for using the Internet.

- You can use the telephone at the same time as the Internet - there's no need for a dedicated line.

Not Everyone Needs Broadband

If you don't need to work with large data files, photographs, music and video clips, then you may well settle for a 56K modem, for the time being at least. An ordinary 56K modem connection may be adequate for your needs for searching the Internet for information and sending and receiving e-mails. Depending on your income, £27-£30 a month may seem a lot to spend, although bear in mind that some 56K services can cost as much as £16 per month. Increased competition and availability is likely to cause broadband services to become cheaper in the future.

Introducing Windows XP

What is Windows XP?

After you switch the computer on, it starts up and the screen displays the *Windows Desktop* with various icons and an optional background design. Click the **start** button at the bottom left of the Windows Desktop and up pops the **start** menu, as shown on the left below. In this example, the Windows Desktop is in the background with four icons on the right representing various programs or *software*.

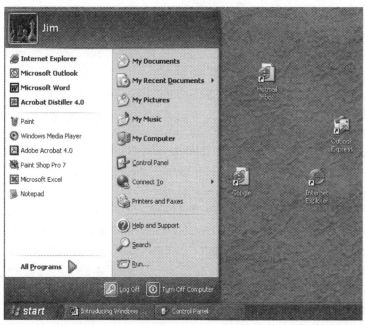

Windows in Control

The *start* menu and the Desktop icons are alternative methods of starting programs and opening documents. They are part of the Microsoft Windows operating system with which we control every aspect of the computer. Microsoft Windows is the *interface* through which we communicate with the computer

During a session at the computer you might select a program from a menu, do some work such as typing a letter, save the letter on disc and print it out on paper. All of these tasks are controlled by Microsoft Windows. The operating system provides the environment in which we control and interact with the computer. It presents the menus from which we select commands or tasks, it controls the screen display and allows us to manage our document files and folders and to save and print our work. The operating system also controls peripheral devices such as scanners and modems and our connection to the Internet.

No matter what task we use our computer for - word processing, "surfing" the Internet, etc. - the operating system will be working away in the background.

Microsoft Windows in various editions has been the dominant operating system on personal computers for many years. Windows XP is the latest version, now installed as standard on most new computers.

Although the work in this book is based on Microsoft Windows XP, most of the material is also applicable to other versions of Windows such as Windows 95,Windows 98, Windows Me, Windows NT and Windows 2000.

A Brief Tour of Windows XP

The next few pages give an overview of some of the main features of Windows XP. Many of the topics are discussed in more detail later in this book. You will see that in addition to providing the software to run your computer, Windows XP also provides a wealth of software tools to maintain the system and carry out modifications. Windows XP also includes many *applications* of its own. Applications are programs which can be bought separately from alternative suppliers, and cover tasks such as browsing the Internet, sending e-mails, drawing and painting, editing text and working with music and video.

Starting Windows XP

When you switch the computer on, you may notice that Windows XP starts up more quickly than earlier versions of Windows such as Windows 98. If the computer has been set up for several people to use, select your user name from the list of users and if necessary enter your password.

This gives you access to your own secure area of the computer, personalised with your own preferred settings.

Launching Programs

The *start* Menu

All of the programs and Windows features can be launched from the *start* menu. Frequently used programs are listed on the left-hand panel and the rest can be started after clicking **All Programs** at the bottom left.

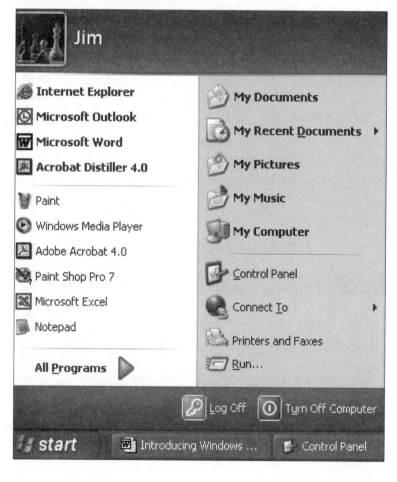

Shortcut Icons

As shown below, you can place your own icons on the Windows Desktop. These icons, known as *shortcuts*, allow you to launch your favourite programs quickly by double-clicking the icon with the mouse.

Shown below are four icons all leading to important programs used in connection with the Internet.

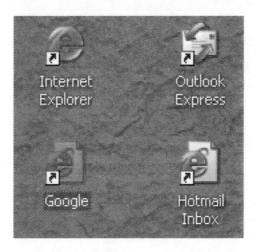

Outlook Express and **Internet Explorer** are part of Microsoft Windows and their icons may appear on the Windows Desktop automatically. **Google** and **Hotmail Inbox** are additional Internet features which I have installed later.

When you install a new piece of software, an icon is often placed on the Windows Desktop. Otherwise it's a simple matter to create a shortcut icon as discussed later.

The All Programs Menu

The main bulk of your programs, however, are launched by selecting **start** and **All Programs**, as shown below. The programs listed on the **All Programs** menu shown below are a mixture of the software applications you have installed (such as your favourite word processing or painting package) together with a vast range of software applications and tools provided by Windows XP.

When a new piece of software is installed, its name will be added to the **All Programs** menu. During the installation process you may be asked if you would like a shortcut icon to be placed on the Windows Desktop. Otherwise you can add the shortcut yourself, as discussed later in this book.

Internet Explorer

This is a program built into Microsoft Windows XP and used to display Web pages. You move between different Web sites by clicking on special *links*. These are pieces of text or pictures which have been programmed to connect to other Web sites when you click on them.

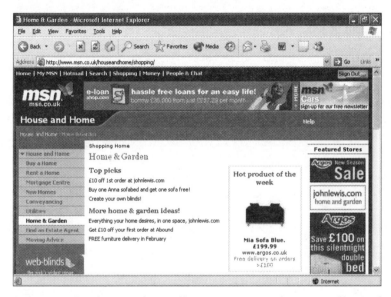

Internet Explorer also allows you to keep a list of *bookmarks* or **Favorites**. These are links to Web sites that you are likely to visit again in the future.

Keyword Searches

You can use Internet Explorer to search the Internet for information using keywords such as "Hardy Perennials". However, special search programs (known as *search engines*) are often preferred, Google being one of the most powerful and popular. Google can be used from within the Internet Explorer program, as discussed later.

Outlook Express

This is the e-mail program included in Microsoft Windows. It is usually started from a shortcut icon on the Windows Desktop or from the **All Programs** menu off the *start* menu.

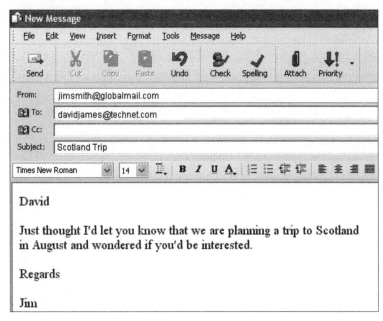

E-mail is very easy to use. Your own e-mail address is entered in the **From:** slot. Your recipient's e-mail address is entered in the **To:** slot. A suitable title must be entered in the **Subject:** slot. After typing the message, click the **Send** button and your message will reach its destination anywhere in the world in no time at all. Please note that you can format your message with different fonts or sizes and styles of lettering and different layouts. Setting up and using e-mail, including your own e-mail address and password, is discussed in detail later in this book.

My Computer

Referring to the extract from the *start* menu shown below, **My Computer** listed in the right-hand panel is a very important tool used in the management of your computer

Clicking **My Computer** in the above *start* menu brings up the window shown below.

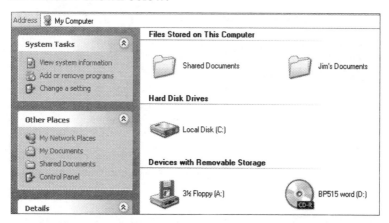

My Computer allows you to look at the resources on your computer, such as disc drives and CDs. You can also carry out maintenance tasks such as cleaning up your hard disc by deleting unwanted files. When you click on the icon for

the hard disc drive as shown above, the panel at the bottom left of the **My Computer** window displays the amount of free hard disc space, as shown on the right.

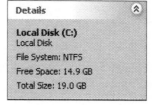

The Windows Explorer

The Windows Explorer (not to be confused with *Internet Explorer*) displays all of the folders and files on your computer. It is one of the main ways to locate a piece of work (usually called a file). Then the document can be opened in the program which created it. The Windows Explorer lists all of the resources of your computer (disc drives, folders, sub-folders, etc.) in a list down the left-hand side of the screen, as shown below.

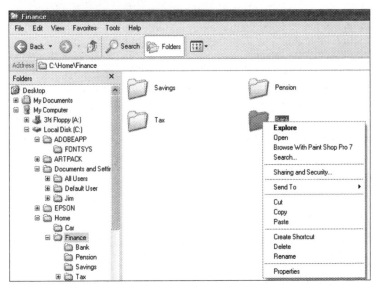

The right-hand panel above shows the contents of any folders you have selected in the left-hand panel.

You can carry out a variety of management tasks on the folders and files listed in Explorer by right-clicking over the appropriate name or icon. This produces a menu as shown above on the lower right.

Amongst other things, the menu includes options to copy, delete, rename and create a shortcut to a file or folder from the Windows XP Desktop.

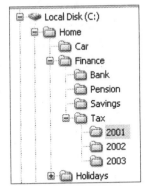

A *hierarchy* of folders is shown in the extract from the Windows Explorer on the left. I have created a folder called **Home**, then within it there are sub-folders of **Car**, **Finance** and **Holidays**. Within the **Finance** folder there are sub-folders **Bank**, **Pension**, **Savings** and **Tax**. Within the **Tax** folder there are sub-folders for years **2001**, **2002** and **2003**. Shown below is an example of a file saved in a sub-folder. The filename is **Letter about tax.doc** and it has been saved in the sub-folder **2001**. The full route to the file down through the various folders is known as the *path*. You can see the path given in the **Address** bar below, i.e. **C:\Home\Finance\Tax\2001**. C: refers to the hard disc drive, **Home** is my main folder and **Finance**, **Tax** and **2001** are the various sub-folders.

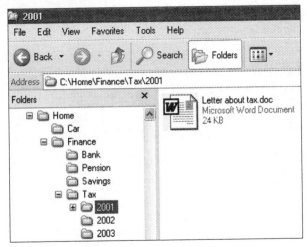

The Control Panel

This is an essential component of Windows XP, used (amongst other things) for altering settings and adding and removing new software and hardware, such as a modem.

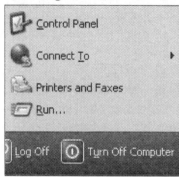

The **Control Panel** can be launched by clicking its name in the *start* menu, shown on the left.

Alternatively click **Change a setting** in the **System Tasks** menu on the left of the **My Computer** window. The **Control Panel** opens in the **Category View** shown below. This view shows the tasks, under broad headings, which can be performed using the **Control Panel**.

Selecting, for example, **Network and Internet Connections** as shown above, leads to some more specific tasks for you to choose from, shown on the next page.

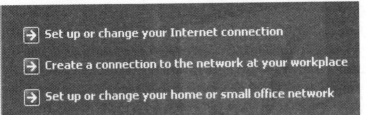

Earlier versions of Windows showed the Control Panel as a set of icons representing the various tools. This arrangement, now known as Classic View, is still available in Windows XP. Classic View can be selected by clicking the option **Switch to Classic View** in the Control Panel in Category View shown at the bottom of the previous page.

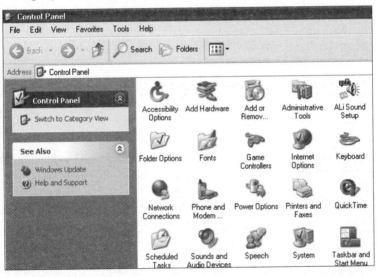

For example, double-clicking the **Phone and Modem Options** icon shown above and on the right allows you to have a look at your modem and check that it's working correctly.

 Phone and Modem Options

If there is a problem with the modem, there is a **Troubleshoot** feature, accessed via a button, as shown on the **Modem Properties** window below. This should help you to solve any problems.

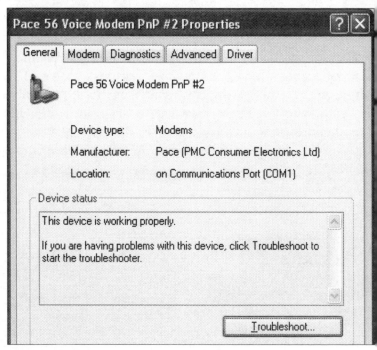

The troubleshooter tries to diagnose a fault in a modem in response to a series of questions.

Deleting Files - The Recycle Bin

This is a container for your deleted files and folders. When you delete a file by pressing the **Delete** key over the file name in the Windows Explorer or My Computer, the file is initially sent to the Recycle Bin. Files and folders in the Recycle Bin are still taking up space on your hard disc.

The **Recycle Bin** is launched by double-clicking its icon on

the Windows XP Desktop. From here the files can be permanently deleted. Alternatively, files in the **Recycle Bin** which have not yet been permanently deleted can still be restored to their original location on the hard disc.

Windows Update

Both views of the Control Panel also give access to **Windows Update**, as shown on the left below.

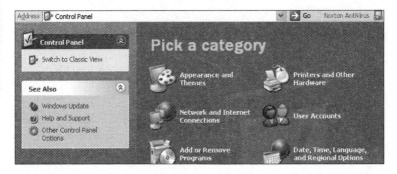

Clicking this option connects your computer to the Internet. Here you are given the opportunity to download from the Internet the latest upgrades available for the Windows software installed on your computer.

Windows Keyboards

You can buy special Microsoft Internet keyboards for a few pounds. These have extra keys programmed to carry out specific Internet and Windows tasks, as an alternative to pointing and clicking with the mouse.

Microsoft®
Internet Keyboard

Easy One-Touch Access to the
Internet, E-mail, and More

These include a group of circular keys along the top of the keyboard for connecting to the Internet and e-mail, also searching, launching the **Favorites** feature and moving **Forward** and **Back** through Web pages. There are also two keys bearing the Windows logo. Pressing either of these takes you straight to the Windows *start* menu, discussed earlier. A further group of three keys open the **My Computer** feature discussed earlier, display an on-screen **Calculator** and put the computer into **Sleep** mode.

Help for Users With Special Needs

Introduction

Microsoft Windows XP contains a number of features to help users with impairments in any of the following:

- Vision
- Hearing
- Mobility

The special needs features in Windows XP are fairly basic and some users with special needs may require more specialised accessibility software. However, the tools included in Windows XP are free and should help some users with special needs to get more out of their computer and the Internet. The features are launched by selecting *start*, **All Programs**, **Accessories** and **Accessibility**.

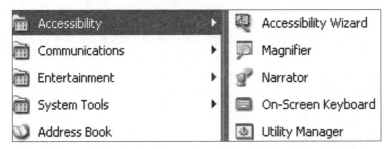

The next section looks at the five **Accessibility** options, shown in the right-hand panel above.

The Accessibility Wizard

A wizard is a program which leads you through a series of interactive screens. The user makes selections from various choices before clicking **Next** to move on to the next screen. Wizards are frequently used in Microsoft Windows for setting up new hardware and software.

Start the **Accessibility Wizard** by clicking *start*, **All Programs**, **Accessories** and **Accessibility**. First you see the **Accessibility Welcome Screen** and on clicking **Next** you are given the option to select a larger text size.

Further dialogue boxes in the wizard allow you to increase the text size which appears in windows title bars and also to increase the size of scroll bars.

Then you are asked to specify your own special needs, by ticking the check boxes for conditions which apply to you.

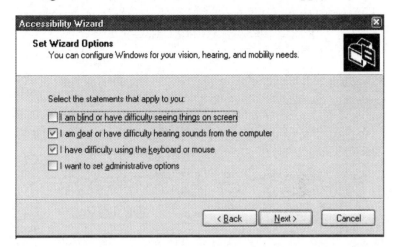

The Accessibility Wizard then proceeds in one of several ways, depending on the ticks you have placed in the above check boxes. For example, if your vision is impaired, the option to display large icons is presented, as shown below.

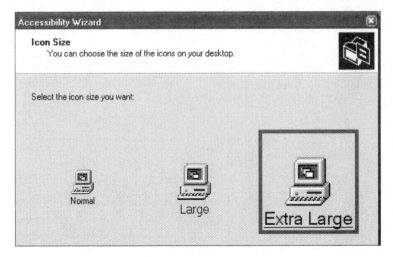

Another dialogue box allows you to select a high contrast colour display and this is followed by a box giving a choice of various colours and sizes of *mouse cursor*.

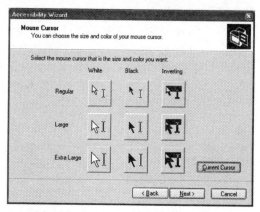

If you have difficulty using a mouse, the numeric keypad on the right of the keyboard can be used instead. For example, the cursor can be controlled by the arrow keys, a mouse-click is replaced by pressing the number **5** key and double-clicking is replaced by the + key. Finally a dialogue box appears allowing you to swap the function of the left and right mouse buttons, to work with your preferred hand.

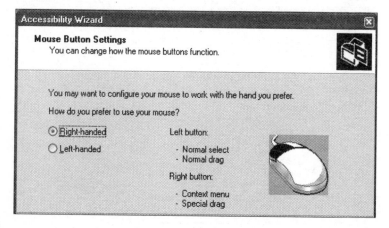

After completing all of the dialogue boxes, click **Finish** to leave the Accessibility Wizard. Please note that you can also set the **Accessibility Options** without using the Wizard. First enter the **Control Panel** from the *start* menu. Make sure the **Control Panel** is in **Classic View**. If the **Control Panel** is currently in **Category View**, click **Switch to Classic View** from the top left-hand corner of the **Control Panel**.

Now double-click the icon for **Accessibility Options**. The following dialogue box opens. A series of tabs (**Keyboard, Sound, Display**, etc.) give access to many further options.

The Magnifier

This feature enables the person with impaired vision to enlarge different areas of the screen, as required. The Magnifier is started by clicking *start*, **All Programs**, **Accessories**, **Accessibility** and **Magnifier**, as shown below.

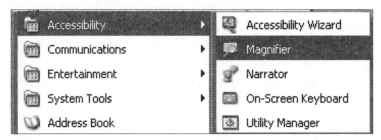

A settings dialogue box also appears, giving you the option to change the magnification level in the range 1 to 9.

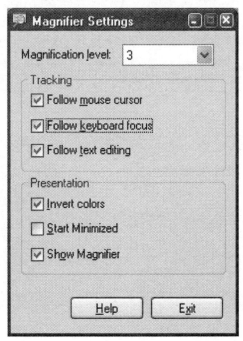

You are presented with a note stating that the Magnifier is intended for users with slight visual impairment. Those with more serious visual problems may need a program with higher functionality.

Note in the dialogue box on the previous page, you can set the magnifier to follow the mouse cursor and the keyboard focus. You can also invert colours to make the screen easier to read. The magnifier appears in its own window above the normal screen. As you move about the normal screen, the magnifier tracks the cursor or keyboard and displays the local text and graphics enlarged, as if viewed through a magnifying glass. Shown below is a screenshot from Microsoft Internet Explorer, with the magnifier running. The area of the screen around the current position is shown magnified across the top of the screen.

The Narrator

If your computer is fitted with a sound card and speakers, the Narrator can read out the text in menus and describe features such as buttons in dialogue boxes. The Narrator can also read out the letters and keys pressed as you type them into a document. To start the program, select **start**, **All Programs**, **Accessories**, **Accessibility** and **Narrator**.

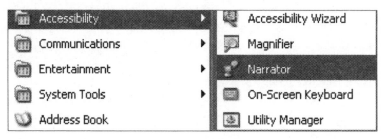

After clicking **Narrator**, an introductory window appears informing you that **Narrator** only works in English and may not work well with certain software. The user is also referred to the Microsoft Web site for details of other "screen reader" software. After clicking **OK** a dialogue box appears allowing the various options to be set in Narrator.

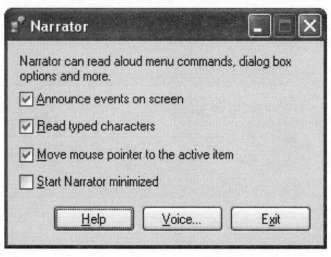

The On-Screen Keyboard

This feature is intended for anyone with mobility problems, who finds it difficult to handle a normal keyboard. The **On-Screen Keyboard** is launched from *start*, **All Programs**, **Accessories**, **Accessibility** and **On-Screen Keyboard**.

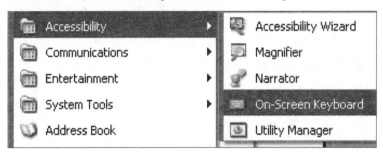

The on-screen keyboard is operated by a mouse or perhaps another type of pointing device. The cursor is moved over the required letter and the mouse is clicked, causing the letter to appear on the page at the current cursor position.

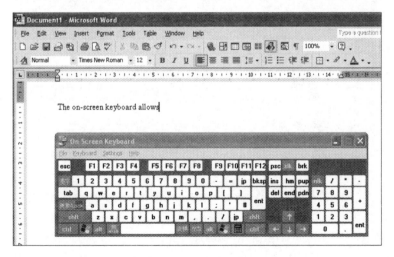

The Utility Manager

The **Utility Manager** is started from *start*, **All Programs**, **Accessories**, **Accessibility** and **Utility Manager**.

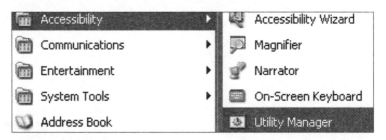

A dialogue box appears showing, within a single window, the special needs programs which are currently running. Here the programs can be started, stopped or configured.

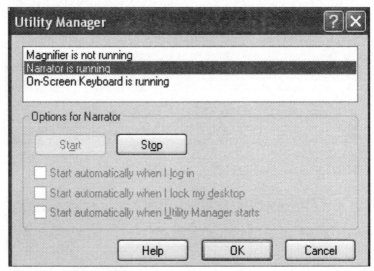

The previous pages describe the special needs features provided free within Windows XP. The Microsoft Web site gives details of additional specialist software and hardware resources to help users with a range of impairments.

Internet Service Providers

Introduction

The Internet Service Providers (ISPs) are companies which host your connection to the Internet. They enable you to set up a *user name* and *password* and provide a telephone number which a 56K modem dials to make a connection to their Internet *server* computer. A server is a computer which stores Web pages and there are millions of servers around the world. Many ISPs also provide connections for the latest broadband services, in which case a telephone number is not required.

The ISP provides a gateway allowing you to search through the millions of Web pages forming the Internet, stored on server computers all over the world. The Internet Service Provider also hosts your e-mail and allocates your e-mail address. Some Internet Service Providers set aside space on their servers to store any Web pages you create.

In addition to the basic Internet functions mentioned above, some ISPs, such as America Online (AOL) and The Microsoft Network (MSN), also act as Online Services. These provide news, entertainment and information pages or *channels*, some of which are only accessible to members subscribing to the service. Currently AOL has 35 million members worldwide, while MSN has 8.7 million.

Typically you pay the Internet Service Providers for their services by a monthly subscription, although there are some "free" connection services. With the free services there may be hidden costs such as expensive telephone support costing as much as 50p or even £1 per minute. You are also likely to be bombarded with a great deal of on-screen advertising. I have been using the free MSN service for some time, where the only cost is for telephone calls at local rates.

The basic MSN service is free, but to connect to it you already need an Internet connection with an Internet Service Provider. The latest free MSN service, MSN Explorer, includes a redesigned Web browser, instant messaging and e-mail. Connecting to the free MSN service is described in the next chapter.

MSN Messenger is a program in which you create a list of your friends who are also members of MSN. Whenever they are online you can communicate with them directly using *instant messaging*, where text messages are exchanged immediately.

At the time of writing, a new subscription service, MSN 8, is being introduced. This will have a subscription charge of £6.99 per month or £59.99 per year. MSN 8 introduces a number of additional features, such as access to the online version of the Encarta Encyclopedia, Microsoft Money and a filter to reduce the number of "junk" e-mails reaching your computer. There are also increased controls so that parents (and grandparents) can protect children from obscene e-mails and Web pages. The homepage of the new MSN Explorer browser is shown below.

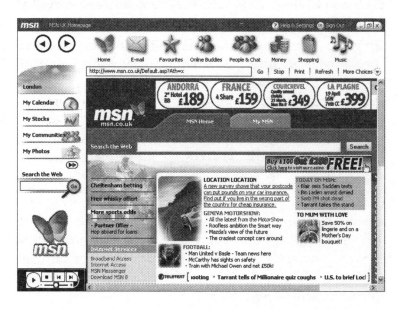

Choosing an Internet Service Provider

The choice of Internet Service Provider can be quite bewildering as there are so many competing offers listing a whole range of complex features. These can regularly be seen in the daily papers and computing magazines, from companies such as AOL, MSN, Freeserve, Tiscali, Demon, Virgin, Supanet, Claranet and UK Online.

It's also a good idea to talk to other people who already have experience of an ISP. Computing magazines such as Computer Active, Web Active and Computer Shopper regularly include comparisons of the different services.

It's fair to say that the big name ISPs, such as those mentioned above, are likely to give a reliable service. Your choice will therefore depend on the extra incentives and features on offer and how they match your individual requirements. For example, ISPs offer differing amounts of free Web space for users to store their own Web pages. This would need to be considered if, say, you wanted to display family photographs on Web pages, to be viewed by friends and relatives around the world. Other ISPs stress the number of information *channels* with their own content such as travel, money and sport, as shown on the left.

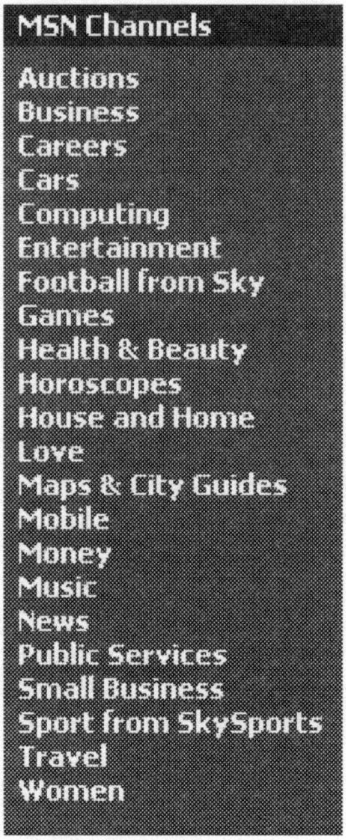

This is perhaps not so important now there is so much information freely available on the wider Internet.

MSN Channels

Auctions
Business
Careers
Cars
Computing
Entertainment
Football from Sky
Games
Health & Beauty
Horoscopes
House and Home
Love
Maps & City Guides
Mobile
Money
Music
News
Public Services
Small Business
Sport from SkySports
Travel
Women

Free Trial CDs

You can obtain free trial CDs from many of the big Internet Service Providers, allowing you to "try before you buy". The free CDs can be picked up in large stores, on the front of computer magazines and through the post to your home. If your modem and computer are working correctly, the CD will connect your computer to the Internet easily and quickly, as described in the next chapter. The free trial may be as much as 120 hours. However, if at the end of the trial period you don't wish to continue with the ISP, you must:

- Cancel the account (usually by telephone or in writing), otherwise charges will continue to be added your credit card.
- Delete the ISP's software, as this may clash with other programs on your computer.

The ISP List in the Network Connection Wizard

If you use the **Network Connection Wizard** described in the next chapter, one of the options is to choose an Internet Service Provider from a list of ISPs available in your area. This not only lists the ISPs, but also gives a summary of the services offered, as shown in the right-hand panel below.

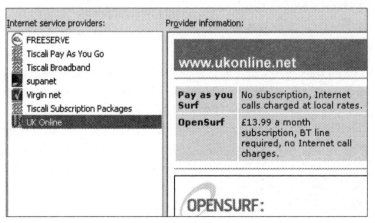

In the Freeserve information below, the all-important telephone support number is given and this should be noted. You are also informed that calls cost 50 p a minute.

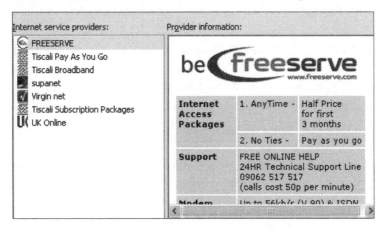

Broadband Services

At the time of writing, many of the ISPs are promoting the new broadband service, discussed elsewhere in this book. While offering very much greater speed for surfing the Web and sending and receiving large files across the Internet, broadband is more expensive. Broadband may not be desirable for those with a limited budget or with only basic Internet usage, as discussed later in this chapter.

The Supanet right-hand panel in the list of ISPs in the **New Connection Wizard** also includes the **Minimum System Requirements** needed to use the Supanet broadband service, shown on the next page. This is the minimum specification of computer considered capable of giving a satisfactory performance with Supanet broadband.

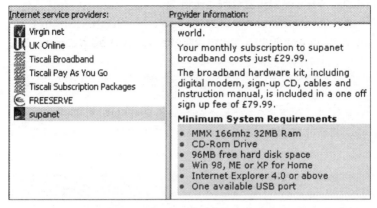

Some ISPs are offering free or reduced price broadband modems and waiving the usual initial connection charge.

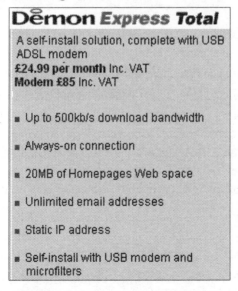

There is competition between ISPs to offer the best content in terms of film trailers, music videos and cartoons. Broadband is designed for such applications, which are too demanding for the traditional 56K modem.

The Cost of Internet Access

There are various packages available from most of the Internet Service providers and these basically depend on how much you intend to use the Internet.

If you already have access to the Internet, perhaps using a friend's computer or through a library, etc., you might wish to look at the Web pages of various ISPs similar to the Tiscali page above. For a list of UK Internet Service Providers have a look at:

www.ispreview.co.uk

Here you can obtain the names of lots of ISPs together with some top ten lists based on the number of subscribers, readers opinions and ISP Review's own research. There are also links to the various ISPs' own Web sites.

Choosing a Package

The package you choose really depends on how much you intend to use the Internet and for what purpose. You might also be constrained by your available monthly budget. The various packages can be summarized as follows:

1. Pay as You Go

This is suitable for the light user of the Internet (perhaps 1-2 hours per week of e-mail and Web surfing). With this package you do not pay a monthly subscription. You only pay for telephone charges (at local rates) for the time you spend online.

2. Unlimited Access

This is suitable for frequent users of the Internet. A fixed monthly subscription (usually about £15) is paid for round-the-clock access. There are no charges for the telephone calls to the Internet. A cheaper version of this package (perhaps £6-£12 monthly) limits the access to off-peak hours such as evening and weekends.

3. Broadband

As discussed elsewhere in this book, anyone wanting a high speed Internet connection to send and receive large files should go for a broadband service. Large files would include film and video clips, music, large graphics files and photographs sent as attachments to e-mails (discussed later in this book). Broadband subscription charges at the time of writing are in the range £20-£30 per month, but this usually includes *unlimited access* and there are no charges for using the telephone line for Internet access. Increased competition should reduce broadband charges in the future.

Criteria for Choosing an ISP

The following list of criteria may be helpful when choosing an Internet Service Provider:

• Speed and reliability connecting to the Internet.
• Telephone access numbers available at *local* telephone rates (does not apply to broadband).
• Free trial periods launched from easy-to-use CDs.
• The monthly or yearly subscription charges.
• The number of e-mail addresses per account.
• The quality and cost of telephone support.
• Support for the latest broadband technology.
• In the case of services providing channels with their own content, the quality and quantity of the pages of information - news, sport, travel, weather, etc.
• The amount of Web space provided free for subscribers to create their own Web sites.
• Protection from viruses in e-mails and file downloads.
• Filters to remove "junk" mail.
• Parental (and grandparents') control over children's access to inappropriate Web sites.

Next

Having decided on the type of package which best suits your needs, the next task is to connect your computer to the Internet. This is covered in the next chapter. As mentioned earlier, the **New Connection Wizard**, which is part of Microsoft Windows, also provides a list of ISPs available in your area. The list includes further details of each ISP and leads to the sign-up process, if you decide to open an Internet account with an ISP on the list.

6

Making the Connection

Introduction

This chapter assumes that you have a modern computer fitted with a 56K modem or an alternative broadband device. If your computer doesn't have a modem at all or your machine has an older modem (say 14.4Kbps), then you ought to get at least a 56K modem fitted. If you don't wish to get involved in the technicalities of modems, then any good computer shop or local specialist will fit one for you and make sure it's working. Alternatively, you may wish to know more about the subject and perhaps fit a modem yourself - it's not that difficult. In this case, the last chapter in this book, entitled "More About Modems", covers the subject in some detail.

In order to use the Internet you will need:

- A recent computer with a correctly functioning 56K modem or alternatively a broadband device.

- An account set up with an Internet Service Provider.

- Internet *browser* software, such as Internet Explorer, a component of Microsoft Windows.

- A telephone line or a suitable cable line.

Going Online to an Internet Service Provider

This section assumes your computer is fitted with a functional modem and is running Microsoft Windows with a Web browser such as Microsoft Internet Explorer. There are several ways to make a new connection with an Internet Service Provider. All of them require you to provide the same basic information, i.e. your name and address, telephone number and credit card details.

During the creation of the new connection you will set up a *User Name*, i.e. the name you use to log on to the Internet. You will also create or be assigned a unique *Password* and one or more *E-mail Addresses*.

There are two common ways to launch the process of connecting to an Internet Service Provider. You can use a free CD from the Internet Service Provider or you can use the **New Connection Wizard** in Windows XP.

Creating an Internet Connection Using a Free CD

Place the CD in the drive and wait for it to start up automatically (a process known as "autobooting").

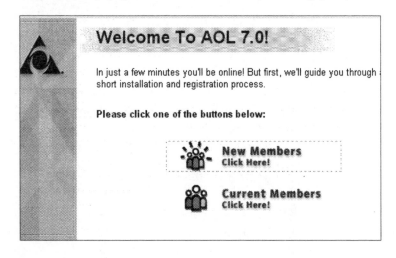

Welcome To AOL 7.0!

In just a few minutes you'll be online! But first, we'll guide you through short installation and registration process.

Please click one of the buttons below:

New Members
Click Here!

Current Members
Click Here!

You will be asked to enter a temporary User Name (sometimes also called a *User ID* or a *Reg Number*). You may also be asked to enter a temporary password. This temporary information is normally printed on the cardboard case of the free CD. With this information you will be able to connect to the ISP. Then you will be asked to enter certain personal information and credit card details. You should also be able to set up your own personal User Name and Password to replace the temporary ones used to make the initial connection. During this process you will also set up an e-mail address.

At some point the telephone number to use for cancelling the new Internet account should be displayed. You may wish to note this number, particularly if you are evaluating a service during a free trial. If you don't want to continue with the service at the end of the free trial period, the onus is on you to cancel it - otherwise payments will start to be charged to your credit card account.

Using the Windows New Connection Wizard

If you haven't obtained a free CD you can use the **New Connection Wizard** in Windows XP to obtain a list of ISPs in your area. Then choose an ISP and complete the new connection by entering all of your details on-line. The process can be started by launching the **New Connection Wizard** from **start**, **Connect To**, **Show all connections** and **Create a new connection**, as shown below.

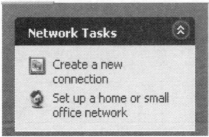

The **New Connection Wizard Welcome** screen appears as shown below.

On clicking **Next**, the wizard presents a choice of the types of connection shown below.

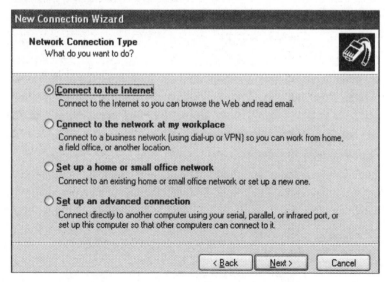

After selecting **Connect to the Internet** and clicking **Next** you are asked to choose a method by which to set up your Internet account.

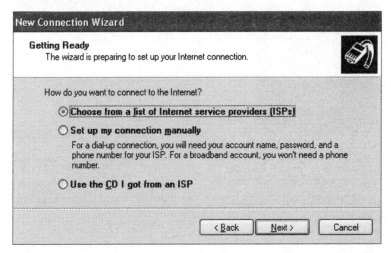

If you do not yet know which Internet Service Provider to use, select the first option, **Choose from a list of Internet service providers (ISPs)**. This involves connecting to the Microsoft Internet Referral Service for a choice of Internet Service Providers in your area.

If you have already arranged an account with an ISP and know your *account/user name*, *password* and *dial-up phone number* for the ISP, then choose the second option, **Set up my connection manually**. Note that if you are setting up a broadband account, a phone number is not necessary.

The third choice, **Use the CD I got from an ISP** has already been discussed. These CDs can often be picked free in large stores, in computing magazines or in the post as unsolicited mail. Just place the CD in the drive, wait for it to boot up then follow the instructions on the screen.

6 Making the Connection

To choose from a list of ISPs available in your area click **Next** and you are given the choice shown below.

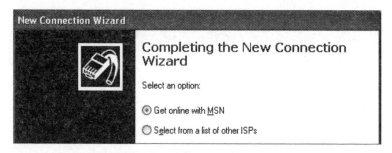

Choosing the first option above will take you straight to the sign-up for the Microsoft Network. Taking the second option above and clicking the **Finish** button will present the two shortcut icons shown below.

If you now double-click **Refer me to more Internet Service Providers**, your computer will dial-up the Microsoft Internet Referral Service, as shown below.

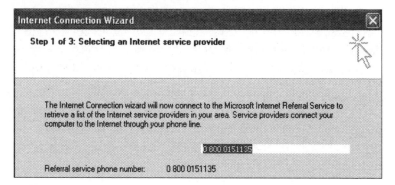

Choosing from a List of Internet Service Providers

A list of Internet Service Providers available in your area is given, with details of their services.

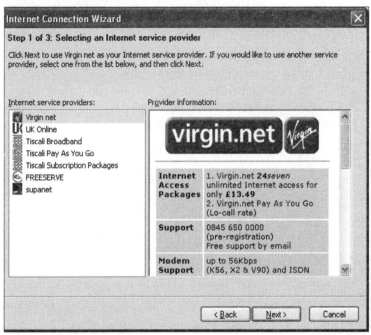

If you click the name of an ISP listed in the left-hand panel, the details of their various services appear in the right-hand panel. The support telephone number of your chosen ISP should also be listed in the right-hand panel shown previously. This is worth noting in case you have any problems.

If you select one of the ISPs in the left-hand panel above, then click **Next**, you are presented with a form requesting your name and address, etc., as shown on the next page.

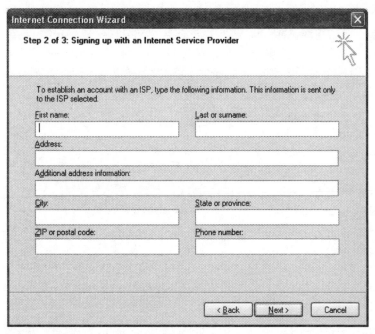

After completing the form you will be connected to the server computer of your chosen ISP, where your personal *User Name*, *Password* and *E-mail Address* are set up. You will also be required to give your credit card details. You may be asked to choose, from a list, the phone number which your modem will dial to connect to your ISP.

- **Check with your telephone company (such as BT, etc.) that all Internet connections using this number will be charged at the *local rate*.**

- **If you're a BT subscriber, you might wish to add your ISP's phone number to your list of BT Friends and Family frequently-used numbers attracting discounts.**

Getting Online with MSN

MSN or The Microsoft Network is a free service and is one of the choices in the list of ISPs in the **New Connection Wizard** discussed earlier. Start the **New Connection Wizard** as described on page 65 onwards. MSN has a separate icon as discussed on page 68 and shown again below for convenience.

 Get online with MSN
Shortcut
2 KB

 Refer me to more Internet
Service Providers
Shortcut

When you double-click the above icon labelled **Get online with MSN,** you are presented with a welcome screen, which also introduces the Web browser MSN Explorer, rather than Internet Explorer. The welcome screen describes some of the available activities on MSN, such as shopping and listening to music.

Welcome to MSN Explorer

MSN® Explorer is the all-in-one software that makes it easy for you to get more from the Web. Browsing the Internet, communicating with friends, managing finances, listening to music, shopping and all your other favorites are a snap with this friendly package tailored for you! You need an existing Internet connection to use this software.

If you are using a modem, make sure that it is connected to the phone line and turned on.

On clicking the **Continue** button at the bottom of the screen, you are told that you will be connected to the Internet using your default connection. This means your computer must already have a dial-up Internet connection set up, with a User Name, Password and the telephone number of an Internet Service Provider.

Your computer then connects to the Internet and you give details of any existing e-mail addresses or click **Create a new e-mail address for me**, as shown below.

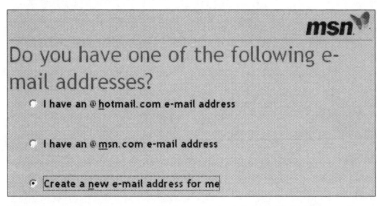

The next few screens ask for personal information such as your name, location (such as England), postcode, date of birth and occupation. After a screen in which you either accept or decline the **MSN Terms of Use** agreement, those accepting are asked to create a password.

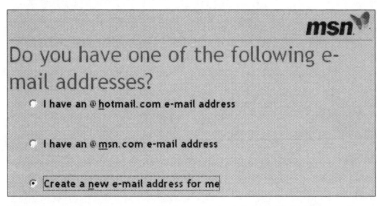

The password has to be retyped to make sure it is what you intended. As an additional security measure you must also provide a secret question and a corresponding answer. The secret question can be chosen from a drop-down menu which appears when you click the down arrow shown in the previous screenshot, to the right of **Secret Question**.

To finish the MSN connection process you need to choose your e-mail name, which will be used as part of your e-mail address, by anyone sending you an e-mail.

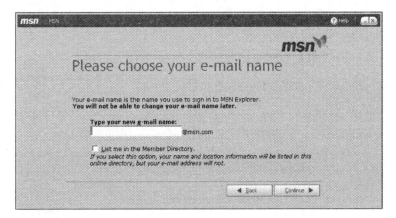

An MSN e-mail address would be something like:

lesleywalker@msn.com

On clicking **Continue** the final screen welcomes you to MSN, thanks you for signing up and confirms your new e-mail address.

Connecting to the Internet Manually

Before starting to set up the connection you will need the following information from your Internet Service Provider:

- User Name
- Password
- Telephone Number for connecting to your ISP.

Please note that a *broadband* connection doesn't need a telephone number.

This work is carried out after starting the **New Connection Wizard** as described on page 65 to 67. For convenience it is described again briefly below.

Select **start**, **Connect To**, **Show all connections** and **Create a new connection**. After clicking **Next** at the Welcome screen then selecting **Connect to the Internet**, on clicking **Next** again you are presented with the choice shown below.

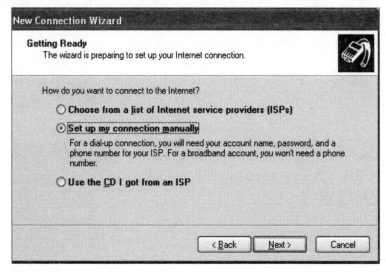

Select **Set up my connection manually**, as shown above.

On clicking **Next** you are asked to choose between a dial-up modem and two types of broadband connection.

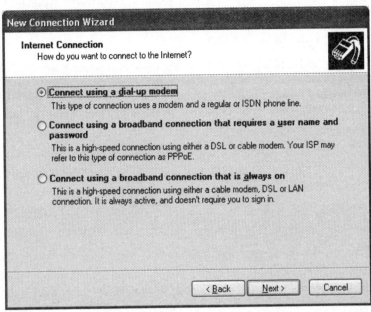

If you have a traditional 56K modem, select **Connect using a dial-up modem**. This leads to a dialogue box requesting the name of your Internet Service Provider. This is followed by another dialogue box requesting the telephone number to be dialled to connect to your ISP.

New Connection Wizard

Phone Number to Dial
What is your ISP's phone number?

Type the phone number below.

Phone number:

You might need to include a "1" or the area code, or both. If you are not sure you need the extra numbers, dial the phone number on your telephone. If you hear a modem sound, the number dialed is correct.

After supplying the ISP telephone number and clicking **Next**, you must fill in your account details as shown below, which must have been previously arranged with your ISP. This essential information may have been supplied either by telephone or in writing.

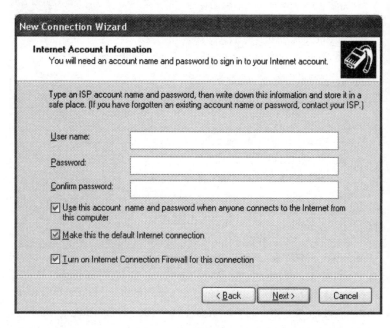

Notice above that **Make this the default Internet connection** is switched on. This means that if several Internet connections have been set up on your computer, the default connection is dialled automatically when you connect to the Internet.

Switching on the Internet Connection Firewall

Make sure **Turn on Internet Connection Firewall for this connection** shown in the previous screenshot is switched on. A *firewall* is a software device intended to prevent malicious "hackers" gaining access to your computer via the Internet. This is increasingly necessary for the new broadband connections which can be "always on", allowing the hackers more time to gain entry to your system.

Broadband Connections

The three connection options shown on page 75 include two broadband connection methods. The second option, **Connect using a broadband connection that requires a user name and password** leads to dialogue boxes requesting your ISP name and then the **Internet Account Information** dialogue box shown on page 76. Apart from the fact that no ISP telephone number is required, this method is the same as for the 56K modem described on pages 75 and 76.

If you select **Connect using a broadband connection that is always on** from the dialogue box shown on page 75, the following window appears.

The previous window informs you that your Internet Connection should already be set up (since for this "always on" broadband you don't need a user name, password or telephone number. There is also a link, **broadband connections**, to information about broadband if you are having problems.

Finishing Off

The following applies to all of the methods of connecting to the Internet, previously described. Click **Finish** and the **New Connection Wizard** is closed and the new connection is created. You should be able to connect to your chosen Internet Service Provider in order to "surf" the Internet and send and receive e-mails, as discussed later.

Checking a Dial-up Connection

If you have created a connection for a 56K modem, you can check the connection as follows. Select *start*, **Control Panel** (in **Classic View**) and double-click **Network Connections** as shown below.

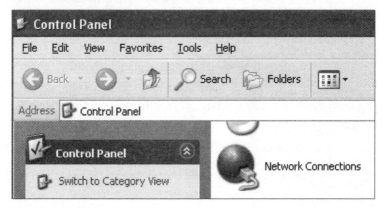

You should see your new connection displayed as shown on the next page.

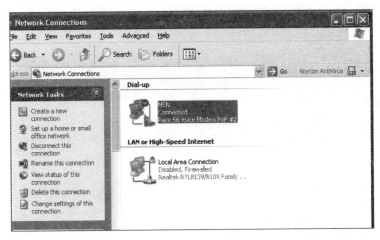

The dial-up connection is shown above. (The **Local Area Connection** also shown above is for a small network connecting my two computers together by a cable and some network expansion cards.)

If you double-click your Internet connection as shown right as **MSN**, your computer and modem should dial-up and connect to your Internet

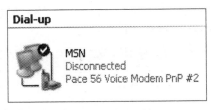

Service Provider. If the icon label changes from **Disconnected** to **Connected** you know your modem is working correctly.

When you launch your Web browser program such as
Internet Explorer it will use your new dial-up connection.

If you have more than one dial-up connection, it will use
the one set as *default*, indicated by a tick on the icon, as
shown on the previous page. Alternatively, you can select a
different connection from the drop-down menu accessed
from the down arrow to the right of **Connect to:** above.

Note that there are options to type in a different **User name**
and **Password**. Please note that, as shown above, the
password can be saved so that you don't have to keep
typing it in. **Connect automatically** avoids the need to click
the **Connect** button.

Changing Your Connection Settings

Select *start*, **Control Panel** (in **Classic View**) and double-click **Network Connections** and highlight your dial-up connection as shown below.

Now click **Change settings of this connection**. The following window appears allowing you to change the dial-up telephone number for your modem connection.

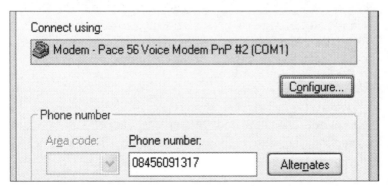

If you click the **Advanced** tab on the previous window, you have can switch the Internet Connection Firewall on or off.

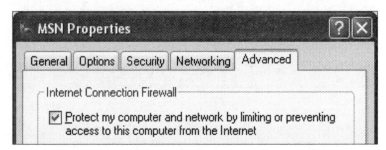

Finally you can make alterations to the settings of your Internet connections by *right-clicking* over the icon in the **Network Connections** window shown below. This displays the popup menu shown on the right below.

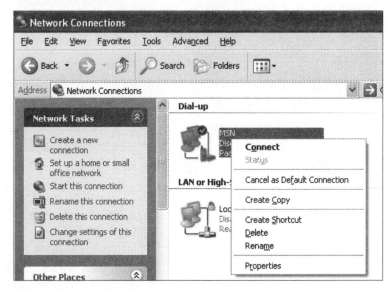

This menu can be used to set (or cancel) the default connection, i.e. the connection to be used automatically when your Web browser program is launched.

Using a Web Browser

Introduction

A *browser* is a program used to view Web pages. When you connect to the Internet you are normally directed to the *home page* of your Internet Service Provider, displayed in your browser. From here you can branch to other Web pages, either by clicking on special *links* or by entering the *address* of another Web page. The browser also allows you to *search* for pages containing certain information. Microsoft Windows includes its own browser, Internet Explorer, which appears on the **start** menu, shown below.

This chapter is based on the Internet Explorer Web browser, but there are alternatives such as Netscape Navigator. To launch the browser, click *start*, then **Internet Explorer**, as shown on the previous page. If you are using a 56K modem, your computer should dial-up and connect to your Internet Service Provider, as discussed in the last chapter.

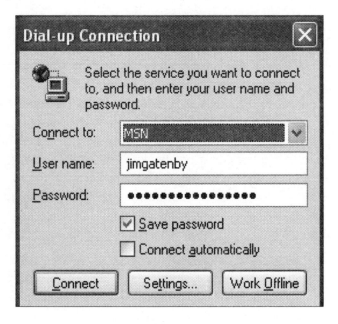

Click in the box next to **Connect automatically** or click the **Connect** button. Connecting to a broadband system is a simpler process.

Work Offline shown above allows you to revisit previously viewed Web pages, while not connected to the Internet. (When you browse the Web, some pages are saved on your own computer for future reference.)

As shown below, once connected the screen will display the home page of your Internet Service Provider. However, it's possible to set your computer to start up and display a different home page of your own and this is discussed later.

In the main body of the MSN home page shown above are various news items, with a rolling list of the latest news stories. There is also a list of **MSN Channels**, providing information on a range of subjects as shown above and on the right.

Around the Web page are various advertisements which can be clicked to yield more information.

Clickable Links

As you move the cursor about a Web page you will notice that the cursor sometimes changes from an arrow to a hand. If this happens over a piece of text, the text changes colour  and is also underlined, as shown on the MSN **Football from Sky** channel on the left and on the previous page. Whenever the hand appears on the screen, this means the cursor is over a clickable *link* (or *hyperlink*) to another Web page. Pictures are also used as links to other Web pages. Links allow you to move from page to page on the Internet, between different pages on the current Web site. Alternatively a link may lead to pages on a totally different Web site stored on a server on the other side of the world.

The Toolbar

After you have moved between several pages, you may want to retrace your steps at some point. The Toolbar across the top of Internet Explorer has a number of icons which help you to "surf the Net".

For example, as shown above, there are buttons to move **Forward** and **Back** through previously visited Web pages.

The **Stop** button shown above is used when a Web page is taking too long to load and you suspect a fault.

The **Refresh** button on the Toolbar, as shown on the right, is clicked if a message appears saying a Web page cannot be displayed. You can also click **Refresh** to make sure your browser is displaying the latest version of a Web page, since some pages are updated from time to time. If you have been viewing previously visited Web pages while working *offline* (i.e. not connected to the Internet), the **Refresh** button can be used to start the reconnection process. The **Connect** window appears as shown below.

Towards the middle of the Toolbar there is the **Home** icon to return you to your home page. Three more icons towards the right of the Toolbar can be used to search for information and to revisit Web pages that you have already viewed.

These are **Search**, **Favorites**, and **History** shown right. These features are discussed in more detail shortly.

If you prefer using a keyboard to a mouse, special *Microsoft Internet keyboards* are available. These have extra keys which are programmed to carry out most of the above Toolbar functions for surfing the Internet.

Using the Address Bar to Connect to a Web Site

To use this method of finding a Web site, you obviously need to obtain the address first, perhaps from an advertisement, or newspaper article. Every Web site has a unique address, such as **http://www.mycompany.co.uk**/. This can be entered manually into the **Address** bar of the Web browser, as shown below.

In computing jargon, the address of a Web site is known as a *URL* or *Uniform Resource Locator*. In the above example, the meanings of the parts of the address are as follows:

http:

HyperText Transfer Protocol. This is a set of rules used by Web servers. **ftp** is another protocol used for transferring files across the Internet.

www

This means the site is part of the World Wide Web.

mycompany

This is the name of the company or organization hosting the Web site on its server computer.

co

This denotes a Web site owned by a UK company.

Other common *domains* (as these address extensions are known) include:

com   Company or Commercial organisation

edu   Education

org   Non-profit making organization

gov   Government

net   Internet company

In addition, some Web addresses include the code for the country, such as **fr** and **uk** as in:

www.bbc.co.uk/

If you know the address of a Web site, enter this into the address bar at the top of the Web browser as shown below. (In practice you can miss out the **http://** part of the address.)

When you click the **Go** button or press **Enter** your browser should connect to the  Web site and display its home page on the screen. Then you can start moving about the site using the links within the page as described earlier. If you click the downward pointing arrowhead to the left of the **Go** button shown above, a drop-down menu appears with a list of the addresses of your recently visited Web sites. If you click one of the addresses it will be placed in the **Address** bar and you can then connect to the Web site by clicking **Go**.

Web Sites of Special Interest

There are many Web sites containing useful information for older people. The following Web addresses can be typed straight into your **Address** bar. There's no need to enter **http://** every time. Most of the Web sites give advice and information on topics such as health, insurance, travel and finance for the over 50s.

www.ace.org.uk   Age Concern Web Site.

www.active-for-life.com Preventing falls.

www.agepositive.gov.uk Focus on skills and ability, not age.

www.antiques-info.co.uk Guide to antiques in the UK.

www.arp.org.uk Association of Retired Persons over 50.

www.ask.co.uk Ask Jeeves search program that answers your questions.

www.bettergovernmentforolderpeople.gov.uk

www.caredirect.gov.uk Information and help for older people.

www.cennet.co.uk Lifestyles for the over 50s.

www.cornhilldirect.co.uk Insurance for the over 50s.

www.dwp.gov.uk Advice on benefit entitlement.

www.fifthmoon.com Advice on money, pensions, business.

www.grandparents-federation.org.uk Support and advice.

www.hairnet.co.uk Internet training for the over 50s.

www.helptheaged.org.uk

www.kelkoo.co.uk Price checks on Internet goods for sale.

www.laterlife.com Promotes a fuller life for the over 50s.

www.moneysupermarket.com Comparisons of savings accounts and loans.

www.neighbourhoodwatch.net Schemes for home security.

www.nhsdirect.nhs.uk Advice and help with illness.

www.opin.org.uk Older People's Information Network.

www.saga.co.uk Wide range of services for older people.

www.ship-ltd.co.uk Release capital tied up in your home.

www.tesco.com Supermarket shopping.

www.theoldie.co.uk A witty magazine for *all* ages.

www.thewillsite.co.uk Help in making your own will.

www.tradingstandards.gov.uk Advice on consumer rights.

www.travel55.co.uk Holidays for older people.

www.uswitch.com Finds cheapest gas, electricity and phone suppliers in your area.

Keyword Searches

If you don't know the address of a particular Web page or you want to find information about a particular subject, you can carry out a *keyword search*. Suppose you want to find information about badgers. The word **badgers** would be entered into the **Search the Web** bar in the browser, as shown below.

After clicking the **Search** button the browser will produce a list of links to Web sites containing the word **badgers**.

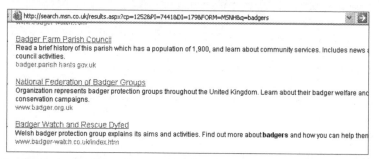

In the results list shown above, the links to the different Web sites are shown underlined and in a different colour.

The name of the Web site is also displayed as shown on the right. Click a link in the

> Badger Watch and Rescue Dyfed
> Welsh badger protection group explains
> www.badger-watch.co.uk/index.htm

results list and your browser will open the corresponding Web page.

Narrowing Down a Search

When you carry out a search, the list of results may include many Web sites which are not relevant. For example, our search for badgers, the small animals, also yields a lot of links to business Web sites that use the word **badgers** in their name. A search can be narrowed down by using extra keywords in the search bar. For example, in the previous example we might enter both **badgers** and **animals** in the **Search** bar.

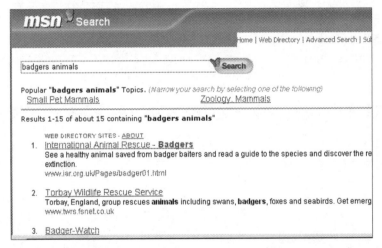

After repeating the search with the extra keyword **animals**, the results contain much more relevant information as shown above. With practice you can make your searches much more successful by the use of additional keywords.

Another tactic to narrow down a search is to enclose your keywords in inverted commas, as in **"Michael Darwin"**, for example. The inverted commas ensure that the names **Michael** and **Darwin** must be next to each other on the Web page. If inverted commas are not included, your results may include *thousands* of irrelevant Web sites containing the separate words **Michael** and **Darwin**, as shown below.

> **Darwin**'s Black Box by **Michael** Behe: A Brief Review
> ... Darwin's Black Box by **Michael** Behe: A Brief Review ... **Darwin** admitted:
> existed which could not possibly have been formed ...
> users.colloquium.co.uk/~BARRETT/Darwin.htm

So far we have looked at the search program built into Microsoft Windows. Such programs are known as *search engines* and many alternatives are available, amongst the most popular being Google from Stanford University.

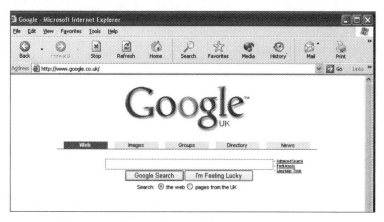

You can start using Google by entering the following in the address bar of your browser:

www.google.co.uk

Your Own Searches

You can find lots of information for older people on the Internet. For example, when you enter **over 50s** in the **Search** bar in Internet Explorer, the following results appear.

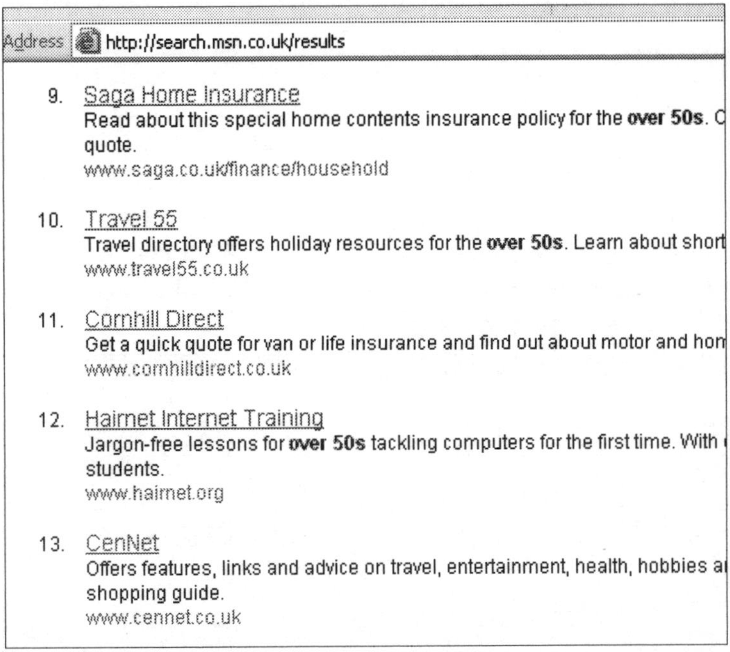

Address http://search.msn.co.uk/results

9. Saga Home Insurance
    Read about this special home contents insurance policy for the **over 50s**. O
    quote.
    www.saga.co.uk/finance/household

10. Travel 55
    Travel directory offers holiday resources for the **over 50s**. Learn about short
    www.travel55.co.uk

11. Cornhill Direct
    Get a quick quote for van or life insurance and find out about motor and hom
    www.cornhilldirect.co.uk

12. Hairnet Internet Training
    Jargon-free lessons for **over 50s** tackling computers for the first time. With
    students.
    www.hairnet.org

13. CenNet
    Offers features, links and advice on travel, entertainment, health, hobbies ar
    shopping guide.
    www.cennet.co.uk

Hairnet listed above is an organisation specializing in Internet and computer training for older people, including tutors who will visit your own home.

You might also carry out similar keyword searches by entering, for example, **retired** or **older people** in your search bar. Then click on the links which appear in the results list as shown above.

Revisiting Web Sites - Favorites or Bookmarks

If you find a Web site which you think may be useful in future, a link to the site can be saved after clicking the **Favorites** icon on the Toolbar in Internet Explorer. (Alternatively you can use the **Favorites** menu on the menu bar shown below).

Favorites save you the task of typing what may be a lengthy URL (www...., etc.,) into the **Address** bar. After you select **Favorites**, a panel opens on the left of the screen, showing a list of Web sites.

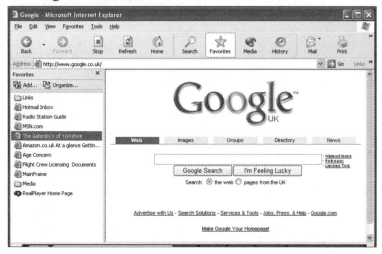

To place the current Web site on your list of **Favorites** click the **Add...** button shown above. In this case I am adding Google to my list of **Favorites**. A dialogue box opens up as shown on the next page.

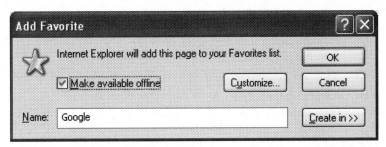

Note in the **Add Favorite** dialogue box above, you can insert a name of your own if you wish. There is also a check box to tick if you want the Web pages to be viewable offline.

After you have added a Web site to your **Favorites** list, to return to the Web site at a later date, click the **Favorites** icon, then click the name of the Web site in the list. The Web site will open on the screen if is available offline. If the Web site is not available offline you will be given the chance to connect to the Internet to view the site online.

Links to sites you have visited in recent days are also recorded automatically in the **History** feature, discussed next.

The History Feature

The **History** feature is a list of links to the Web sites you have visited in recent days. As discussed later in this chapter, you can set the number of days for which links are kept. To have a look at your **History** list click the icon on the right of the Internet Explorer Toolbar shown right and below.

The History feature opens up in a panel on the left of the screen as shown below.

Click on a day to reveal the links for that day. Then click a link to connect to the site.

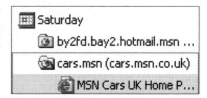

If you are working *offline*, some of the Web pages may be available without connecting to the Internet. Otherwise, if a page is not available, you will be invited to connect to the Internet to view the Web page online.

As mentioned earlier you can set the number of days to keep links in the **History** feature. From the menu bar along the top of Internet Explorer, select **Tools** and **Internet Options....** The **Internet Options** dialogue box opens up with the **General** tab selected, as shown below.

At the bottom of the **Internet Options** dialogue box shown previously is a small box for setting the number of days to keep links in the **History** feature. As shown below there is also a button to clear the entries in the **History** feature.

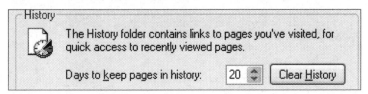

At the top of the **Internet Options** dialogue box shown on the previous page is a box which allows you to change your **Home page**. As mentioned earlier, this is the page which your browser normally opens on connection to the Internet.

To change your **Home page**, type a new entry in the **Address:** bar as shown above.

While working on the Internet, a lot of *temporary files* are saved on your hard disc. These can be safely removed using the two **Delete** buttons shown below, which appear in the middle of the **Internet Options** dialogue box shown on the previous page.

Saving Information from Web Pages

Previous pages in this chapter discussed the way the *links* to Web pages can be saved using **Favorites,** also known as *bookmarks.* These allow you to log on to the Internet and reconnect to a Web site visited previously. In some cases Web pages are saved on your hard disc so that you can view them offline in **Favorites.** It is also possible to manually save Web pages or just parts of them on your hard disc. Then the information saved on your hard disc can be used in various ways. For example:

- Copy and paste the information into a word processing document, as part of a report or presentation.

- Send a Web a page to a friend or colleague as an e-mail attachment.

- Print a copy of the information on paper to show other people, away from the computer.

Saving a Web Page to Your Hard Disc

When you are connected to the Internet, with the required page displayed on the screen in Internet Explorer, select **File** and **Save As....** It's a good idea to create a new folder for your Web pages, using the **Create New Folder** icon in the **Save Web Page** dialogue box shown below.

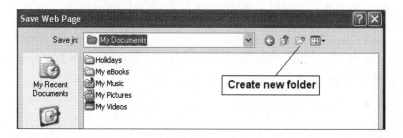

File name:	MSN UK Homepage	⌄	Save
Save as type:	Web Page, complete (*.htm;*.html)	⌄	Cancel
Encoding:	Web Page, complete (*.htm;*.html)		
	Web Archive, single file (*.mht)		
	Web Page, HTML only (*.htm;*.html)		
	Text File (*.txt)		

Then enter a name for the file and select from one of several file formats in **Save as type:** as shown in the extract from the **Save Web page** dialogue box shown above and on the previous page. These file types include:

Web Page, complete (*.htm, *.html)

This format saves everything on the page, i.e. text, graphics files and any sound files, etc.

Web Archive, single file (*.mht)

This takes a snapshot of the Web page and saves it as a single file.

Web Page, HTML only (*.htm, *.html)

This option saves only the text, in HTML format.

Web pages saved in the above formats can be viewed offline at a later date, in a browser such as Internet Explorer or Netscape Navigator. (The browser can be set to work offline using the main **File** menu.)

Text File (*.txt)

This is plain text without any of the formatting features built into pages in the HTML language. A **Text File** is universally acceptable to other programs such as word processors and simple text editors like Windows Notepad and WordPad.

Saving a Graphic Image from a Web Page

While connected online to the Internet, with your browser displaying the required Web page:

- *Right-click* over the image to be saved. A menu appears including the option to save the picture in a folder of your choice.

There are also options to create a shortcut from the Windows Desktop to the Web page or to use the picture as a Background on your Windows Desktop.

- Select **Save Picture As:...** from the menu which appears, as shown above. This leads to the **Save Picture** dialogue box shown on the next page. Here you can enter a name for the picture and choose whether to save it in a picture format such as **.bmp** or **.jpeg** (discussed later in this book).

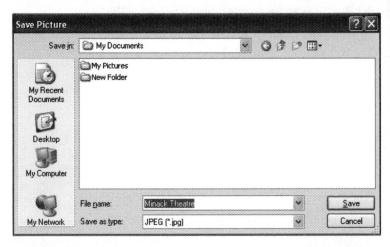

After saving, the picture can be opened for viewing offline. Both **.bmp** and **.jpeg (.jpg)** files can be opened in **Paint**, a program which is supplied as a free accessory to Microsoft Windows. To launch **Paint** select *Start*, **All Programs**, **Accessories** and **Paint**, as shown below.

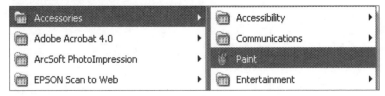

You might also use the highly rated Paint Shop Pro image editing software to view and possibly modify an image copied from the Internet. A copy of the graphic image can easily be printed using **File** and **Print...** from the graphics program.

Saving Part of a Web Page - Cut and Paste

If you only want to copy say a piece of text from a Web page, a simple method is:

- Select the required text on the Web page.

- Click **Edit** and select **Copy** from the menu. This puts a copy of the piece of text onto the **Windows Clipboard**. The *clipboard* is a temporary store for holding text and graphics. It is used when information is copied between different documents.

- Open the destination for the Web page extract. This might be a Microsoft Word document, for example.

- Select **Edit** and **Paste** to place the Web page extract onto the page in the document, which can now be saved and printed, etc.

Printing a Web Page

Internet Explorer has an option to print Web pages. From the menu select **File** and **Print....** Or use the **Print** icon on the Internet Explorer Toolbar. There is also a **Print Preview...** option showing how the pages will print on paper.

Print

Some Web pages print perfectly while you are online to the Internet, while others miss out important information. If you have problems printing while online, try some of the methods described on the previous pages for saving information from Web pages to your hard disc. For example, select all or part of a page then use **Edit** and **Copy** in the browser to place the information on the clipboard, before using **Edit** and **Paste** to put the Web information into a word processor like Microsoft Word. Then you can print the information like any other word processing document.

7   Using a Web Browser

Internet Activities

Introduction

This chapter looks at some of the ways the Internet can be used to help with common tasks. Without exception these online tasks can be carried out more quickly and easily than by traditional methods. Many of these tasks involve the transfer of money over the Internet. Although initially sceptical about the use of the Internet for financial transactions, experience has convinced me of the efficiency and security of these systems. (Internet security is discussed later in this chapter).

The tasks described in this chapter, which it is hoped will be of particular interest to older people, are:

- Arranging Holidays

- Internet Banking

- Internet Security

- Internet Shopping

- Tracing Family History

Arranging Holidays

The traditional way to arrange a holiday is to send off for several brochures. Then after scanning the brochures, to make several telephone calls to check for vacancies and probably make a provisional booking.

Nowadays many hotels and guest houses have their own Web site. With several linked pages, this can provide far more information than an entry in a brochure. Also, the information in the Web site can be *updated* very quickly, while the brochure may not be printed again for several months.

In addition, you need to have a good idea of where you want to go before sending for brochures; with the Internet you can browse through lots of places looking at tourist information and pictures of local amenities. Then you just click on a link to hotels and view the available accommodation, before booking your holiday online.

For example, if considering a holiday in Cornwall, you might type the keyword **Penzance** into your **Search** bar, as described in the last chapter. This particular search produces a list of Web sites, with a link to the site "**Penzance on line**" at the top of the list.

WEB DIRECTORY SITES - ABOUT

1. **Penzance**, Cornwall,
   Explore this historic town in the south-west. There's good detail on the su
   www.penzance.co.uk

2. **Penzance**, England Hotels - Places To Stay
   Reserve a room at **Penzance**, England hotels. Check out hotel amenities
   www.placestostay.com/discount/hotel/united_kingdom/penzance.html?F

As shown above, the Web address of this site is:
www.penzance.co.uk/

If you click the link shown on the | **Penzance**, Cornwall, |
right and on the results list on the
previous page, the **Penzance On line** Web site opens as
shown below.

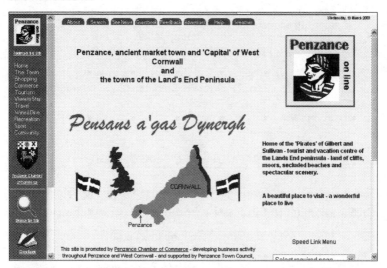

The above site is promoted by the Penzance Chamber of
Commerce and supported by the Penzance Town Council.

The Web site contains many links to
places of interest and amenities in the
town and the surrounding area, as shown
in the enlarged extract on the left.

Select **Where to Stay** and after clicking a
further link to **Hotels**, the list of hotels
shown on the next page appears.

Now we can have a look at the different hotels in Penzance.

Guest Lodge Penzance
   The Promenade, Penzance. Phone: 01736-366882
Lombard House
   Regent Terrace, Penzance. Phone: 01736-364897
Ⓒ **Mount Prospect Hotel**
   Briton's Hill, Penzance. Phone: 01736-363117
Ⓒ **Tarbert Hotel & Restaurant**
   11 Clarence Street, Penzance. Phone: 01736-363758
Warwick House Hotel
   17 Regent Terrace, Penzance. Phone: 01736-363881

Other Hotels

Abbey Hotel
   Abbey Street, Penzance. Phone: 01736-366906

For example, selecting the Tarbert Hotel & Restaurant above takes us to the hotel's home page, shown below.

Tarbert Hotel and Restaurant

Clarence Street, Penzance, Cornwall, TR18 2NU

Tel: +44 (0)1736 363758 Fax: +44 (0)1736 331336

'e mail' reception@tarbert-hotel.co.uk for more details

Tarbert Hotel and Restaurant offers quality accommodation and hospitality. Situated in Penzance, West Cornwall, UK, which is a delightful market town and an ideal centre for touring the area, the Hotel provides B&B or dinner, bed and breakfast for a short break or a longer vacation.

The Hotel is part of a Georgian Terrace of houses which were originally built in 1830 by Harrod Investment Corporation as homes for the Merchant Sea Captains who sailed the world in search exotic goods for Harrod's discerning clientele. The original owner, Ralph Sheldon Kindly was lost at sea in his quest for such treasures.

From the home page there are links to all of the facilities of the hotel and information about the surrounding area, as shown at the top of the next page.

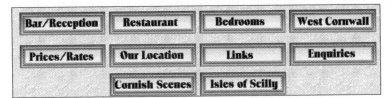

Bar/Reception	Restaurant	Bedrooms	West Cornwall
Prices/Rates	Our Location	Links	Enquiries
	Cornish Scenes	Isles of Scilly	

For example, click **Bedrooms** and samples of the accommodation can be viewed.

A Superior Double Bedroom

You can also have a look at some sample menus.

Pan-fried Sirloin Steak Garni
Baked Chicken Breast stuffed with Leeks, Orange and Bacon
Seared Ostrich steak marinated in Lemon, Garlic and Worcester Sauce
Roast rack of Cornish Lamb accompanied by a Redcurrant, Sherry and Mint Sauce
Roast Monkfish with a White Wine, Saffron and Chive Sauce
Whole Baked Lemon Sole with Citrus Butter
Roast Sea-bass accompanied by a Lemon and Fennel Sauce
Baked Fillet of Cod accompanied by a Sun-dried Tomato and Caper dressing
Roast Lentil and Hazelnut Loaf served with a Pimento and Tomato Sauce (v)
Summer Vegetable Medley with Tagliatelle in a creamy Mustard Sauce (v)
Stuffed Peppers accompanied by a Mushroom and Thyme dressing (v)

Finally you can either make an enquiry or a definite booking after clicking the **Enquiries** button shown on the previous page. First you fill in your personal details as shown in the extract below.

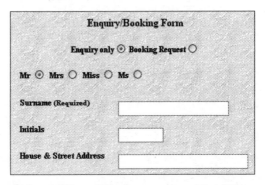

You are also asked to give your *e-mail address* and you then select the date and duration of your holiday and the number and type of rooms required.

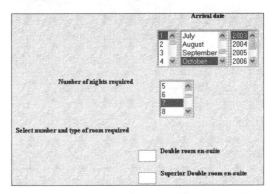

Finally there is a space to enter requirements such as a special diet or ground floor room. The completed Enquiry/Booking Form is then sent to the hotel by clicking the SEND button at the bottom of the form. An e-mail can be quickly returned the same day to confirm your booking.

Finding a Last Minute Holiday

The search program in your Web browser is an invaluable tool for finding holiday information. For example, if you wanted to arrange a last minute holiday, type those three words as the keywords in your **Search** bar as shown below.

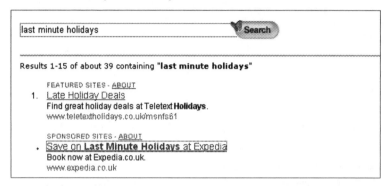

Following the link to Expedia at **www.expedia.co.uk**, shown above, opens up a page of last minute breaks to various European destinations.

Internet Banking

It's now possible to carry out many of your banking activities from the comfort of your own home. There's no longer any need to travel to a branch unless a face-to-face meeting is necessary or you need to withdraw actual cash in the form of notes.

Obviously many people will be concerned about security, but reputable organisations guarantee that in the event of fraud, customers won't lose any money. Internet security is discussed in more detail later, but one of the main security methods is to *encrypt* (or encode) all information sent between your computer and the bank's. Even if the information were fraudulently intercepted it would not be intelligible to the criminals.

To participate in *online banking*, you obviously need a computer and modem and an account with an Internet Service Provider. To find out more about online banking, log on to the Web sites of any of the major banks, such as the Halifax, at **halifax.co.uk** and the Bank of Scotland, at **bankofscotland.co.uk**.

Once online to the bank you will find lots of information about the range of services offered. A major advantage of online banking is that you can access your accounts at almost *any time of the day or night* - there's no need to wait for normal banking hours.

With online banking you will be able to carry out most of the normal banking functions, such as:

- View your balance
- Print a statement
- Pay bills
- Transfer funds between your various accounts
- Transfer money to another person's account
- Set up standing orders
- Apply for an increased overdraft
- Check and cancel direct debits

As shown on the extract from the Halifax site above, there is a link to initiate the opening of an online bank account.

The Web sites for the Halifax and Bank of Scotland both have links leading to demonstrations which give you a tour of the online banking service. The following extract shows a sample of the Account Statement from the Bank of Scotland, where the last 90 days' transactions can be viewed on the screen.

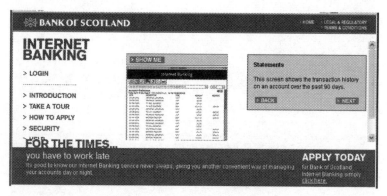

Once you have signed up for online banking, your bank will arrange with you a *user name* (sometimes also called a *login name* or a *user ID*) and a *password*. Shown below is the login screen for the Halifax Online Service.

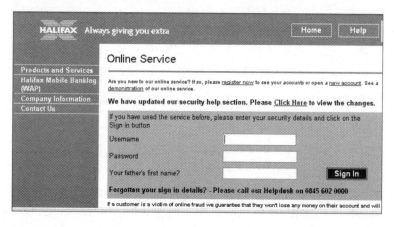

You may be asked to provide at least one additional piece of security information, such as a parent's name, some memorable piece of personal information or a secret question and answer. If you forget your password there is usually a number to ring to arrange a new one. At this time the additional security information is used to prove your identity. Obviously all security information such as passwords, etc., should be kept safe and not written down and left in obvious places.

Once you have opened an online bank account you can view your list of accounts. This gives an overview of your various accounts with the bank, displaying your total financial position on one screen. At the Halifax, this is known as your **Financial Portfolio**, described below.

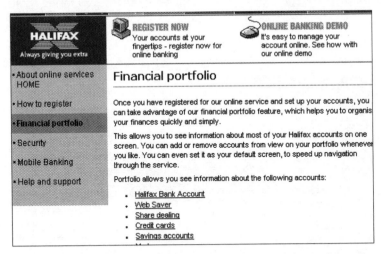

The portfolio lists not only your bank accounts, but also details of any share dealings, investments, mortgages, credit cards and saving accounts, etc.

The **Halifax Financial Portfolio** and the various online services are accessed via the menu shown below.

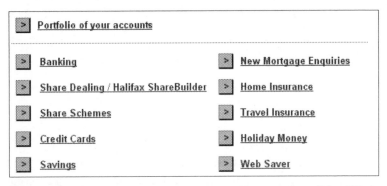

You can also open new accounts, such as the Halifax Web Saver shown below. Internet savings accounts may offer interest rates above those generally available with conventional savings accounts.

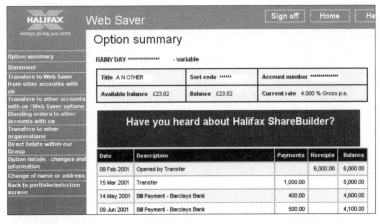

As shown above, although the Web Saver is an investment account, it also enables bills to be paid and money to be transferred to an account with a different bank.

Internet Security

Carrying out financial transactions over the Internet is bound to be a cause for concern. Online banking involves sending and receiving personal financial information between your computer and that of the bank. Internet shopping and paying for goods online, as discussed shortly, requires us to give our credit card details to suppliers. Fortunately, reputable businesses like the big banks and established suppliers have strict security systems to prevent fraud. In the unlikely event of a fraud occurring, the best organizations guarantee that customers won't lose money. There are also many simple precautions which individuals can take to make fraud difficult.

Passwords

As well as a *User Name*, you will be issued with or choose your own *Password*. This should not be something obvious like the name of a pet or family member. Although your password doesn't appear on the screen (usually replaced by a line of dots, etc.), beware of anyone looking over your shoulder while you type it.

- Never leave your password lying around, in fact don't write it down at all.
- Don't walk away and leave the computer open at your bank account. Some systems log you out if the computer is not used for 10 minutes
- Always *log out* or *sign off* when you have finished using the computer.
- Don't give anyone your user name or password.
- Change your password regularly.

Security Software

As discussed elsewhere in this book, make sure your computer has a *firewall* installed. This is a piece of software which stops hackers from gaining access to your computer and possibly interfering with your bank accounts.

A *virus* is a program maliciously designed to invade your computer and cause damage. Some organizations provide their customers with virus protection software. Otherwise *anti-virus software* packages such as Norton AntiVirus, McAfee VirusScan and Dr. Solomon's Anti-Virus Toolkit are relatively inexpensive. Make sure your computer has a firewall and anti-virus software - large companies protect their own *server* computers in the same way.

Secure Servers

Servers are the computers used by banks and other large organizations to hold the details of millions of transactions and customers' accounts. *Secure servers* use *encryption* to prevent criminals from accessing financial or confidential information sent between computers. Encryption scrambles or encodes the information so that it can only be decoded or made intelligible by authorized users.

Organisations such as banks and large suppliers use an encryption level known as *128 bit SSL (Secure Sockets Layer)*. Whenever you are online to a secure server, a small closed padlock icon appears at the bottom right of your screen. Double-click the padlock icon to reveal details of the security certificate issued to the company. Always deal with companies who use secure servers.

Online Shopping

The "dot.com" boom of a few years ago saw the rapid rise and equally rapid fall of numerous companies selling goods and services on the Internet. While many companies disappeared, lots of others have developed successful online businesses. These provide a very quick and easy method of purchasing goods without the need to travel into town. Of course, we are really talking about *online ordering*, since someone still has to physically collect the goods from a warehouse and deliver them to our door.

One of the first major online stores was **Amazon.com** of America, known in the United Kingdom as **Amazon.co.uk**.

Initially being known for selling books, Amazon has now extended its range to include many other products such as music and video, toys and electrical goods such as cameras and computer equipment.

Initially you must set up an account with a password, your name and address and e-mail address.

After logging onto the Amazon site (which you might have placed in your list of **Favorites** or **Bookmarks** for convenience), you browse the categories. For example in the music category there are links down the left-hand side for the different types of music such as **Classical**, **Jazz** or **Pop**.

As shown above, there are options to **Search** the current category by entering a keyword such as an artist's name. When you have found an item of interest, such as a book or CD, there is usually a link to click for more details. In the case of a book this may be the author's synopsis of the contents and customers' reviews of the product. In the case of a music CD the further details would be a list of all of the tracks.

On the Amazon extract shown below, you would click the link **See more product details** to display a list of all the tracks on the CD.

If you intend to buy more than one item, select **Add to Shopping Basket** as shown on the right above. Then further items can be selected and added to the basket. If you only want a single item, it can be bought immediately with *one click* as shown above right as ***Buy Now with 1-Click***. For this latter option you must have already set up an account with your credit card details, your name and address and e-mail address. Then the whole transaction can be completed with no further input from you.

When you finish adding items to your shopping basket you need to click **Proceed to Checkout** to pay for the goods by credit card and give address and credit card details if you are a new customer. You will be informed by e-mail of the progress of your order and when it has been dispatched.

Like the banks mentioned in the previous chapter, Amazon uses a secure server, with encryption of data sent between computers. Amazon also states that no customer has lost money due to fraud when using their system and there is also a security guarantee.

An unusual service offered by Amazon is to *buy back* books previously purchased, which are then offered for sale as used items.

> **J Gatenby**, make £115.14. Sell your past purchases at Amazon.co.uk today.

Supermarket Shopping Online

In principle, the Home Shopping schemes operated by firms like Tesco and Sainsbury are similar to Amazon. Again your credit card details must be provided. At the core of your order is your basic shopping list of items bought regularly, every week, say. Items can be added to the list or removed. Any item which is not in stock may be substituted by the staff with an equivalent item, perhaps of a different brand. Or you can choose not to have substitutions for out of stock items.

Delivery charges are typically in the range £4-£6 depending on the time slot, which you select from a grid of available times. Against this must be considered the saving in your time and transport costs. Ordering a weekly shop online need only take a few minutes. Compare this with the effort involved in a trip to the supermarket. This might take an hour or two including travelling.

In my experience, online shopping is fast, secure and much easier than conventional shopping.

Tracing Your Family History

Many older people decide to research their family records. Much of this work involves searching parish records and contacting relatives using traditional methods of investigation. However, the Internet is a tool which can make the job very much easier and more efficient, when used in combination with traditional methods. If you type the keyword **genealogy** into your search engine you will find a host of Web sites dealing with the subject.

Results 1-15 of about 302 containing **"Genealogy"**

SPONSORED SITES - ABOUT
- **Genealogy**
  Scotland's People is the official government source of genealogical data for Scotland. Register or and dicover your ancestry.
  www.scotlandspeople.gov.uk

- Ancestry.com - Number One **Genealogy** Site
  Research your UK **genealogy** at Ancestry.com - the world's most popular family history site. Search England, Ireland, Scotland and Wales. Search now.
  www.ancestry.com

- Draw up Your Family Tree on Your PC
  This PC software makes it really easy to research and build your own family tree. Use your own s photos.
  www.edream.co.uk

WEB DIRECTORY SITES - ABOUT
1. GENUKI - UK and Ireland **Genealogy**
   Offers a comprehensive guide to researching from abroad, and includes extensive links to docum and search services.
   www.genuki.org.uk

Some of the best known Web sites for this work include:

www.ancestry.com

www.genuki.org.uk

www.genealogy.com

www.familytreemaker.com

www.familyrecords.gov.uk

www.census.pro.gov.uk

www.pro.gov.uk

Many of these sites give access to large databases of family records, births, deaths, marriages, etc., together with general advice on researching your family using both the Internet and traditional methods. Some sites contain the names of specialist researchers who will undertake the work for you.

Some sites, such as **FamilyRecords.gov.uk**, give advice on sources of information such as birth, marriage and death certificates. Then there are pages telling you where to obtain copies by visiting government offices such as the Family Records Centre in London.

The GENUKI Web site is maintained by a charitable organization and provides large data bases of parish and other records for the United Kingdom and Ireland. Advice for newcomers to genealogy is also given.

Some of the genealogy Web sites listed earlier include help and software to compile your own family Web site. Such a site has been created in my own family by Mark Gatenby (**www.gatenby.freeserve.co.uk**) and attracts a large number of visitors making contributions from around the world. There are several different aspects to Mark's site. First there is a family forum which allows you to post messages asking for information about particular relatives. These are available for viewing worldwide

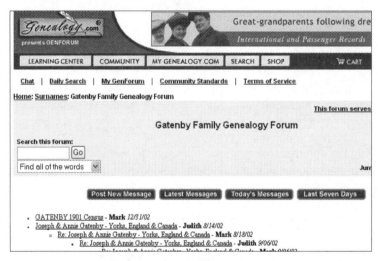

All being well a request for information will result in lots of replies, like the one shown below.

8 Internet Activities

Across the top of Mark's site is a menu bar giving access to family records from around the United Kingdom. The various menus include **Births, Marriages**, various **Censuses, Places** and **Family Trees**.

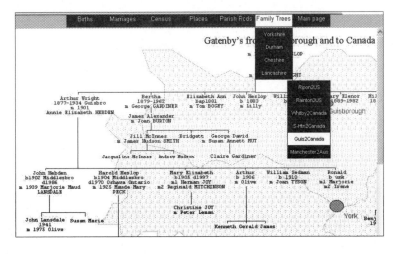

Gatenby	Date			Spouse	Age	Notes
ann	30 September 1795				9m	father carpenter
ann	16 November 1809				2	
ann	22 May 1822				65	
ann	06 October 1833				59	
barbara	06 September 1833				70	
dinah	07 June 1787			john	82	wid john carpenter -
elizabeth	15 April 1763			william		wm carpenter
elizabeth	20 April 1770	ann & late joseph			34	father sailor

The family tree for my own branch of the family is found under the **Overseas** menu, reflecting the exodus of families from Yorkshire to Canada in the last century.

The 1901 Census Online

This is a relatively new site (**www.census.pro.gov.uk**) provided by The National Archives (formerly known as The Public Record Office). The entire records for the 1901 Census for England and Wales have been placed on the Internet, including copies of the original handwritten enumerators' forms. The site was initially overwhelmed with users and facilities had to be greatly increased. You can search using several criteria such as a person's name, a place name or the name of a merchant vessel.

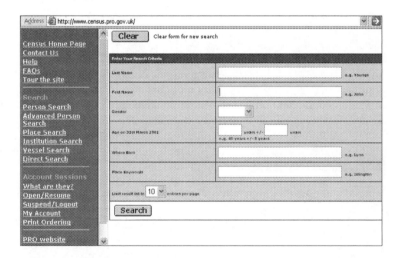

If the search is successful you can open an Account Session with a minimum session charge of £5. You can check in advance the cost of different pieces of information. For example, a transcript of the details of an entire household costs £0.75. Payment may be made by credit card or by the use of vouchers bought in advance from suppliers such as public libraries.

With certain browsers, you can view and print an image of the original handwritten document listing details of every member of a household. Alternatively you can order a copy of the image to be posted to you.

As shown below, you can print out a transcript of the Census form for a household, listing all of the members including name, sex, age, occupation, where born and relationship to the head of the family.

Person Details			
Full Transcription Details for Mary Gatenby View Image/Other Household members			
PRO Reference			
RG Number, Series	Piece	Folio	Page
RG13	4577	79	8
Name			
Mary Gatenby			
Relation to Head of Family	Condition as to Marriage		Age Last Birthday
Head	W		45
Profession or Occupation	Employment Status		
	Undefined		
Where Born	Address		
Yorkshire Kildale	10 Borough Rd West		
Civil Parish	Rural District		
Middlesbro			
Town or Village or Hamlet	Parliamentary Borough or Division		
Middlesbrough	Middlesbro		

The 1901 Census Web Site is available 24 hours a day, 7 days a week.

At the time of writing there are plans to put on the Internet censuses for England and Wales from other years, in addition to the 1901 Census.

Using E-mail

Introduction

E-mail is one of the most popular uses of the Internet. It enables people to communicate rapidly with friends, relatives and colleagues around the world. E-mail has several important advantages over the ordinary post and the telephone, for example:

- An e-mail travels to its destination almost instantly.

- A short message is very cheap to send, only the cost of a *local* telephone call.

- The same e-mail can be sent to several different people by simply clicking their names in an electronic address book.

- An e-mail can be sent at any time of the day or night.

- You don't have to make direct contact with the other person - if they are out they will see your message next time they read their mail.

- An e-mail can be *saved* in a folder or *printed* out.

- You can send *attachments* with e-mails. These can be photographs, sound or video clips or document files containing text or pictures, for example. With the latest broadband technology very large files can be sent extremely quickly.

The E-mail Process - An Overview

Microsoft Windows includes its own e-mail program, called Outlook Express. Such a program, known as an *e-mail client*, allows you to type in new e-mails and to read and store the e-mails sent to you by other people.

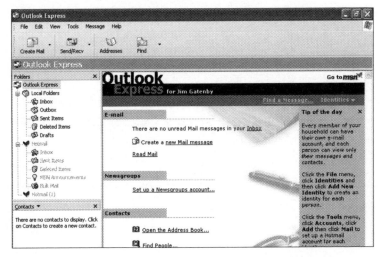

You can create a new e-mail message working *offline*, if you want to reduce connection charges. Click **Create Mail**, as shown above.

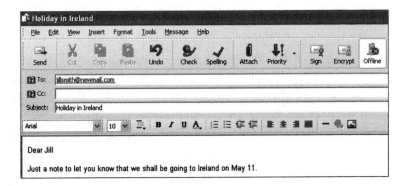

When you've entered your message, along with the e-mail address of your friend and also entered a **Subject**, you would click **Send**. Initially the message will be placed in the **Outbox**, shown below on the right.

As soon as you connect to the Internet and click the **Send/Recv** icon shown right, the message is sent to the mail server of your Internet Service Provider, such as MSN or AOL. A copy of your outgoing message will be kept in the **Sent Items** box on your computer, shown on the right.

Then the message is delivered and stored at the mail server of your friend's Internet Service Provider. Next time your friend reads their e-mail, the new messages are downloaded to the **Inbox** on their computer and saved on their hard disc.

So when you send someone an e-mail, the message is not immediately transmitted to their computer. Although the e-mail may arrive at your friend's ISP mail server in a matter of seconds, it will sit there unread until your friend checks their mailbox. Of course, if you arrange to send important mail to a friend or colleague who is standing by to receive it, the whole process can be completed in a few seconds. Used in this way e-mail is many times faster then conventional methods.

A major feature of e-mail is the sending of *attachments*. These are files of any sort - photos, video clips, text, graphics, sound, etc., which are "clipped" to an e-mail message and

sent along with it. I have used this method to send an entire book to the printers, but using a 56K modem this is not to be recommended. Large files can cause great inconvenience to the person receiving them because of the time needed to download them. However, the arrival of *broadband* Internet technology means very large files can be sent as attachments in a fraction of the time (compared with the time taken when using the traditional 56K modem).

E-mail avoids the expense and inconvenience of packing and posting. Distance is irrelevant - the cost is just the charge for a local phone call.

Another major advantage of e-mail over conventional mail is the ease with which you can send multiple copies to a wide circulation list. You simply select the recipients' names from your electronic address book. If you're involved in confidential work, you can send "blind copies" so that recipients don't know who has received a copy. Shown left are the headers for carbon copies (**Cc:**) and blind carbon copies (**Bcc:**). There are e-mail features to automate the sending of an immediate *reply* to a message and to *forward* a copy of a message to someone else. You can arrange to be automatically notified when someone has read an e-mail that you have sent to them.

E-mails remove much of the clutter of the ordinary letter post on paper, although a hard copy can be printed if necessary. E-mails can be organised efficiently into folders. As shown by the Toolbars below, e-mail programs like Outlook Express allow the text of the message to be formatted with different effects such as fonts, graphics and in the HTML code used in Web pages. E-mails can also include links to Web sites and different "stationery" or background patterns.

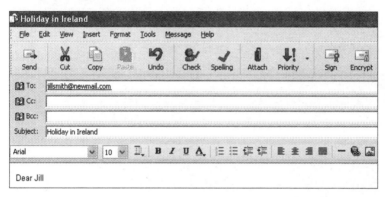

As shown above, Outlook Express also includes icons for "cutting and pasting", i.e. moving text about in an e-mail or pasting in text from other documents. There is also a spelling checker and icons to *digitally sign* and *encrypt* the e-mail for security, discussed in the next chapter.

Many Web sites now include links such as **"Send us an e-mail"**, designed to encourage you to contact them. When you click the link, your e-mail program opens up. The e-mail address for the Web site is inserted automatically. You simply type in the text of the message and click **Send**.

E-mail Requirements

In order to send and receive electronic mail, you need:

- An E-mail Program such as Outlook Express.

- A Connection to the Internet provided by an Internet Service Provider (ISP). This will include a User Name and a Password arranged with your ISP.

- An E-mail Address arranged with your ISP.

- The names of the "mail server" computers which handle the incoming and outgoing mail at your Internet Service Provider. Examples of mail servers are:

  Incoming mail (POP3): pop3.email.msn.com
  Outgoing mail (SMTP): smtp.email.msn.com

Your Internet Service Provider should give you the actual names of your particular Incoming and Outgoing mail servers. The server names listed on this page are for demonstration purposes only.

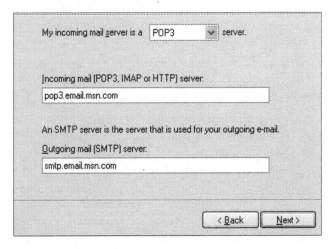

E-mail Addresses

When you sign up for an Internet account you will be able to choose, or be given, your own e-mail address. This is a unique location, enabling your mail to reach you from anywhere in the world.

Common types of e-mail address are shown by the following fictitious examples:

> **stella@aol.com**
>
> **james@msn.com**
>
> **enquiries@wildlife.org.uk**

The part of the address in front of the @ sign is normally your *user* name or Internet *login* name. The second part of the address identifies the mail server at your company, organization or Internet Service Provider. The last part of the address is the type of organisation providing the service. In the above addresses **.com** refers to a commercial company. Common organisation types include:

.edu	Education
.gov	Government
.org	Non-profit making organisation
.co	UK commercial company
.com	Company or commercial organisation
.net	Internet company

A two-digit country code such as **uk** or **fr** may be used at the end of the e-mail address.

Setting Up Outlook Express

Before starting this work, your modem or other connecting device should have a functional connection to an Internet Service Provider (operating at local telephone rates). The ISP should have provided you with all of the necessary information including:

Incoming mail server

Outgoing mail server

User Name

Password

E-mail address.

Outlook Express is the e-mail program provided as part of Microsoft Internet Explorer, installed when Windows was set up on your computer. Launch the program directly from the Windows *start* menu or from *start*, **All Programs** and **Outlook Express**.

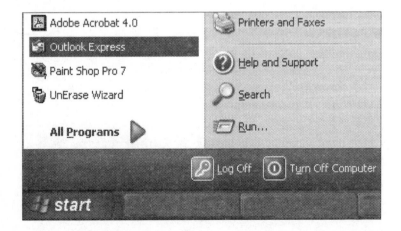

The first task is to create a new e-mail account, initiated by clicking **Tools**, **Accounts...**, **Mail** and **Add**. Now select **Mail...** from the small menu which pops up to start the **Internet Connection Wizard**.

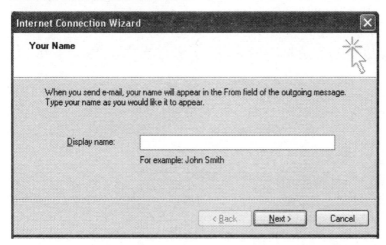

Enter your name as you would like it to be displayed on your outgoing messages, before clicking **Next** to continue.
The next dialogue box requires you to enter your e-mail address, which you should have obtained from your Internet Service Provider.

9   Using E-mail

In this example I am using an e-mail address arranged with Hotmail, Microsoft's free Web-based e-mail service. After clicking **Next** you are asked for details of your *mail servers*, information which must usually be obtained from your **Internet Service Provider**.

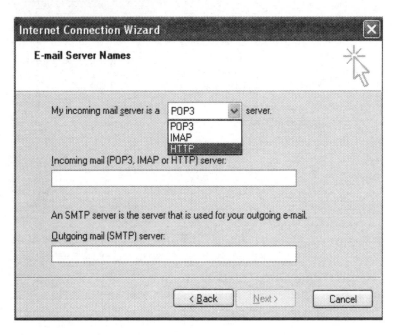

Users of Hotmail will select HTTP for this Web-based service while other users will be using either a POP3 (Post Office Protocol 3) incoming mail server or perhaps an IMAP server. POP3 servers download the mail to your computer while IMAP servers allow you to manage the mail on the server and only download the headers of each message, to save time. The next dialogue box asks for the **Account name** and **Password** which you should have arranged with your Internet Service Provider.

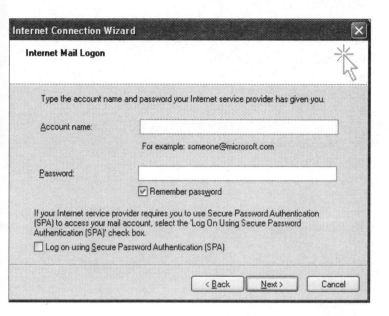

If you are concerned about unauthorized access to your e-mail then remove the tick next to **Remember password**. The final window congratulates you for successfully completing the wizard. Now click **Finish** and you are presented with the **Internet Accounts** window open at the **Mail** tab, as shown below. To create additional e-mail accounts, repeat the previous procedure starting on page 136.

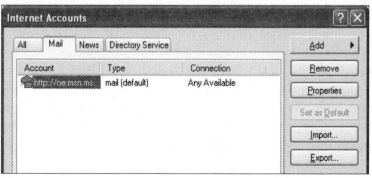

Using Outlook Express

You can test Outlook Express by creating a simple e-mail and sending it to *yourself*. This may seem pointless but it's a quick way to ensure that the system is working. Launch Outlook Express from the *start* menu then click the **Create Mail** icon on the left-hand side of the menu bar. The main message creation window opens ready for you to enter a new message, as shown below.

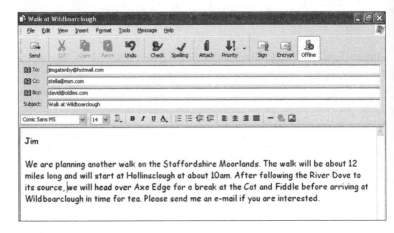

Please note in the screenshot above, showing the message creation window, there are three bars, **To:**, **Cc:** and **Bcc:**, into which recipients' e-mail addresses can be entered. You must enter one or more e-mail addresses or names into the **To:** bar, while **Cc:** and **Bcc:** are optional. Multiple e-mail addresses should be separated with a semi-colon (;). These address bars are discussed on the next page. You must also make an entry in the **Subject:** bar.

Enter the e-mail address(es) of your main recipient(s) in the **To:** slot. Selecting contacts for your e-mail from an electronic address book is discussed shortly. Multiple entries, separated by a semi-colon (;) are allowed.

To send "carbon" copies of the e-mail to additional recipients, list their e-mail addresses in the **Cc:** slot. Anyone whose e- mail address is entered in the **Cc:** bar can see who else has received a copy.

The **Bcc:** slot doesn't appear until you select **View** and **All Headers** from the Outlook Express menus. If you place e-mail addresses in the **Bcc:** slot, these recipients will receive a copy of the message without the other recipients knowing.

Enter a meaningful title in the **Subject:** bar, so that the message can be easily identified at a later date.

Now it's just a case of typing in the text of your message. E-mail programs like Outlook Express have a range of text formatting effects such as different fonts, bold, italic, underlined, centred and justified text and also a spelling checker.

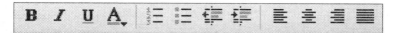

There are security features such as **Sign** allowing a digital signature to be added to the e-mail, ensuring that only authorized people can read the message. **Encrypt** encodes an e-mail so that it can only be decrypted and read by certain people. Security is discussed in the next chapter.

The **Attach** feature allows you to send files such as Word documents along with your e-mail. Please note that the e-mail message on the previous page is being entered *offline*. You can go offline by clicking the **Offline** icon on the right-hand end of the menu bar, shown above. When you're working offline the icon has a white background. The **Priority** icon above allows outgoing messages to be marked **High**, **Normal** or **Low Priority**.

Sending an E-mail

When the message is finished, click the **Send** button. If you are currently working offline you will be informed that the message will be placed in the **Outbox** until you click **Send/Recv**.

If you are working offline and click **Send/Recv**, you will be asked if you want to go online.

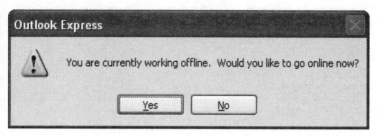

On clicking the **Yes** button, the dial-up connection window will appear allowing you to connect to the Internet. When you are online the new e-mail is sent to the mail server at your recipient's Internet Service Provider. You are informed of progress as the message is sent.

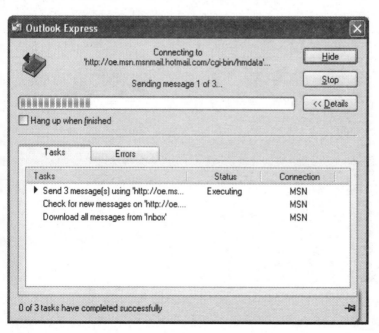

Outlook Express checks for new messages whenever the **Send/Recv** icon is selected.

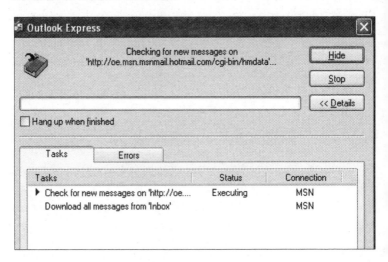

Any new mail which has been sent to you will be downloaded as shown below.

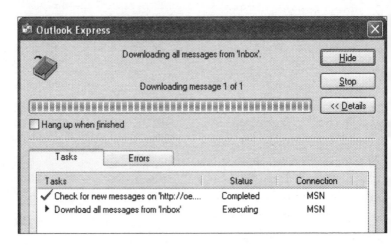

Your e-mail recipients will see your message as soon as they log on and depending on their Internet Service Provider, their mail may be downloaded to the **Inbox** on their own computer.

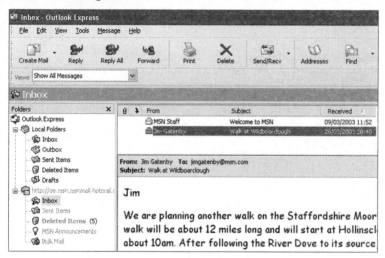

If you are using a Web-based Internet service like Hotmail, there is a duplicate set of Web-based folders as well as the **Local Folders** stored on your own computer's hard disc, as shown above. When you send a message it is initially placed in the **Outbox** in the **Local Folders**. After it has been sent an entry appears in the lower **Sent Items** folder shown right under **http://....** Messages received using the Outlook Express and Hotmail combination can be viewed online or offline from the lower **Inbox** shown above and on the right.

Handling Incoming E-mails

Once you have read the e-mails in your **Inbox**, there are several ways of dealing with them. If the e-mail is not important you will probably want to read it then delete it by highlighting it and pressing the **Delete** key. However, this only sends them to the **Deleted Items** folder, accessed from the left-hand panel of Outlook Express when you select **View, Layout...** and **Outlook Bar**. To empty the **Deleted Items** folder, select **Tools, Options...** and **Maintenance** and make sure **Empty messages from the 'Deleted Items' folder on exit** is switched on. Then click **Apply** and **OK**. As soon as you close Outlook Express, the **Deleted Items** folder will be cleared of messages.

Saving Your E-mails

The e-mails you receive are automatically saved in your **Inbox**. However, this soon becomes cluttered and you'll probably want to store important messages in folders of your own choice. From the **File** menu in Outlook Express, select **Save As....** The **Save Message As** window appears, as shown below, allowing you to save the e-mails with a name of your choice in a folder of your choice.

There is an icon in the **Save Message As** dialogue box, shown right, which allows you to create new folders. This enables you to save your e-mails under different headings

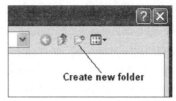

Create new folder

or categories. An e-mail can be saved using the **.eml** extension selected in the **Save as type:** bar shown on the previous page. Alternatively the plain text of the message can be saved as a **Text File** (**.txt**). This can be imported into many programs, such as word processors. You can also save the e-mail message in the **HTML** format (**.htm**, **.html**) used by Web pages.

The saved e-mails can be viewed later by double-clicking on their name or icon in the **Windows Explorer**.

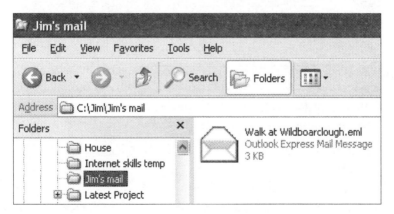

If the file has been saved in the **.eml** format, for example, double-clicking the message as shown above will launch Outlook Express and display the message. Similarly if an e-mail has been saved in the **.htm**/**.html** format, double-clicking the icon for the e-mail will be open the message in your Web browser such as Internet Explorer.

Responding to E-mails

Reply

To send a reply to an e-mail sitting in your **Inbox**, select the e-mail then click the **Reply** button. (Also note

Reply All and **Forward** above). The Outlook Express message window opens up with the name or e-mail address of the sender of the e-mail already entered in the **To:** slot. The **Subject:** slot is automatically infilled with the original subject, preceded by the letters **Re:**.

Note that the reply also includes the text of the original message. This option can be switched off in the **Inbox** of Outlook Express after selecting **Tools**, **Options** and the **Send** tab. Then click the box next to **Include message in reply** to remove the tick, as shown below.

Reply All

Choosing this option ensures that your reply is sent to all of the recipients of the original message, whose names or e-mail addresses are automatically infilled in the **To:** slot. Otherwise **Reply All** is similar to **Reply**, with the option to include the original message with your reply.

Forward

This option allows you to send on a copy of an e-mail to one or more other people. Select the message to be forwarded then enter the e-mail name or addresses in the **To:** slot. Multiple e-mail addresses should be separated by a semi-colon (;). You can also enter a short message of your own to accompany the forwarded message. The **Subject:** slot will be infilled with the original subject, preceded by the letters **Fw:**.

Additional E-mail Features

Introduction

E-mail programs like Outlook Express include several additional features, over and above the basic requirements for sending and receiving e-mails. These include:

- The *Address Book.*
- E-mail *Attachments*, i.e. files sent together with an e-mail.
- *Stationery* to enhance the appearance of an e-mail, including backgrounds.
- *Signatures* to include personalised text on e-mails.
- *Encryption* and *digital* signatures for security.

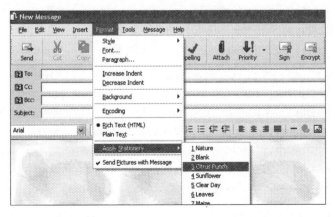

Using the Address Book

This feature can be used to record all of your regular e-mail contacts. Instead of typing their e-mail address every time you send them a message, you simply select their name from the list in the address book. The address book, shown below, can be opened by clicking on its icon on the top of the Outlook Express window, shown right.

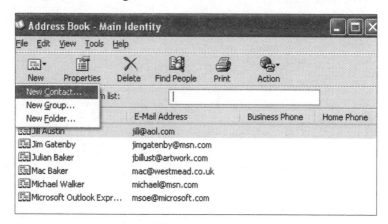

To make a new entry, click **New** then **New Contact...**, etc., as shown above, then type their details in the **Properties** window as shown on the next page.

To add a new individual you would click **New Contact**, while there are also options to organise contacts into a **Group** or a **Folder**. For example, you could set up a group for a gardening club. The group members' names and e-mail addresses would all be listed in the group. To send a message to every member of the group you would only have to select the group name in the address book.

First you complete the **Name** tab shown below, which includes your contact's full name, e-mail address and their nickname, if required.

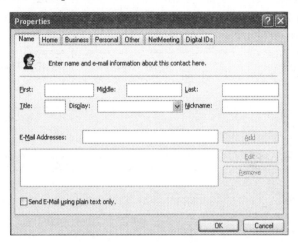

When adding a new contact to the **Address Book**, you can include a great deal of personal, business and family information such as birthdays, anniversaries and children's names, after selecting from various tabs as shown below.

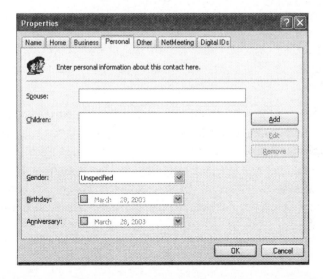

10 Additional E-mail Features

When creating a new message, as discussed on pages 142 and 143, you don't need to manually type the e-mail addresses of contacts already in your address book. Simply 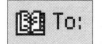 click the address book icon to the left of the **To:** bar, then select their names in the **Select Recipients** window shown below. Click either **To:**, **Cc:** or **Bcc:** from the middle panel as appropriate.

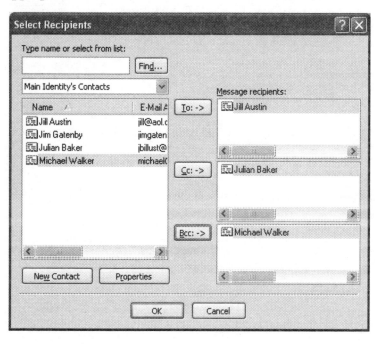

Click **OK** to enter the selected e-mail addresses into the new message. Note that only the *names*, not the e-mail addresses, appear in the **To:** bar as shown below.

Sending E-mails to Members of a Club or Group

This is a useful feature if you regularly want to send an e-mail message to a large group of people. For example, you might be the secretary of a club or society. It would be a waste of time if you had to enter 30 names each time you sent them an e-mail, even if you picked them off your list of contacts in the address book. The answer in Outlook Express is to set up a **Group**, then you only need to select the **Group** name for the e-mail to be sent to every member.

In Outlook Express, open the **Address Book** by clicking its icon.

From the **Address Book** select **New** and **New Group**. The **Properties** dialogue box opens as shown below.

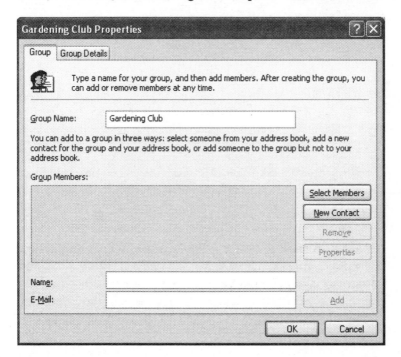

Enter the name of the group in the **Group Name:** bar as shown on the previous page. Members already in your **Address Book** can be added to the group by clicking the **Select Members** button shown on the previous page.

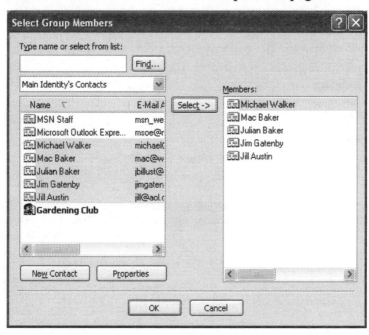

Multiple names can be selected in the left-hand panel by holding down the control key (**Ctrl**) while clicking the left mouse button. Similarly, a *block of names* can be selected by holding down the shift key while clicking. Now click **Select** in the middle panel to place these new members into the group, as shown above. When you click **OK**, the **Gardening Club Properties** window opens up with the group members listed in the **Group Members:** panel, as shown on the next page.

If you wish to add a new member to the group who is not in your address book, click the **New Contact** button above, then enter the details. This method also enters the new contact in your address book as an individual entry. You can also add a new member to the group using the **Name:** and **E-Mail:** bars shown above. This member will be added to the group but will *not* be added to the address book.

Once you have added the members to your group and clicked **OK**, the name of the group appears in your address book alongside of the names of individual contacts. To send e-mails to every group member, simply click the group name in the address book to place them in the **To:** bar of your e-mail.

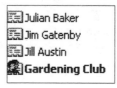

E-mail Attachments

When you send an e-mail message, you can include with it an additional file known as an *attachment*. This can be any sort of file, usually selected from your hard disc. It could, for example, be a word processing document, graphics file, or photograph.

Sending an Attachment

First the text of a new e-mail is entered in the normal way. Then click the **Attach** icon shown left or select **Insert** and **File Attachment...** from the menu bar.

The **Insert Attachment** box opens to allow you to select, from within the folders on your hard disc, the file to be attached to the e-mail.

Clicking the **Attach** button inserts an **Attach:** field, with an icon and file name **Harvest.jpg (1.55MB)** shown below.

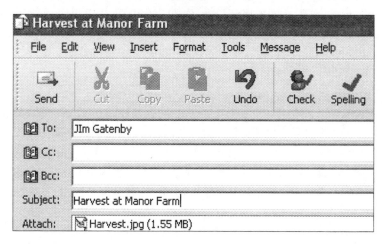

Now click **Send** and the message and its attached file will be sent as a single item.

The photograph **Harvest.jpg (1.55MB)** shown as an attachment above will take a long time to send and download using a *56K modem*. It should only take a few seconds with a *broadband system*. Other types of file such as Word documents and spreadsheets, for example, have much smaller file sizes and can be sent much more quickly. The next section describes how photographs can be effectively reduced in size in Windows XP.

Virus Checking

Any files you send as e-mail attachments should first be checked using an up-to-date anti-virus program, like Norton AntiVirus or Dr. Solomon's Anti-Virus Toolkit. In MSN Hotmail, incoming and outgoing attachments are checked automatically using McAfee VirusScan.

E-mailing Large Photographs

Large photographs can be sent as attachments as shown in the previous screenshot, but they can easily occupy over 1MB. This makes the pictures very slow to send and receive unless you are using a broadband system rather than a 56K modem.

For large photographs there is an alternative method in Windows XP, described below, which drastically reduces the size of the file for the photograph. This makes it much quicker to send the photograph as an attachment.

Before starting work on the e-mail, display the photograph in its folder using the Windows Explorer. The folder might be **My Pictures** or one you have created yourself. Now *right-click* over the photograph you want to send with your e-mail. A menu appears as shown below and in more detail on the next page.

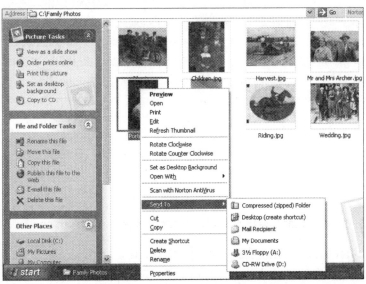

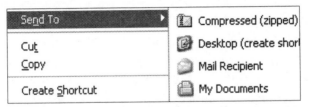

When you select **Send To** and **Mail Recipient** the **Send Pictures via E-Mail** window appears, as shown below.

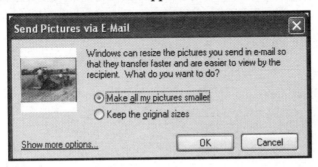

This allows you to make the pictures smaller and therefore faster to send. Now select **OK** and after a short while the photographs will have been reduced in size. Your e-mail program opens up ready for you to enter the text for the message before finally clicking **Send**.

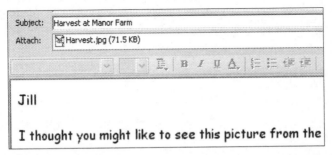

Notice above that the size of the picture has been reduced to **71.5KB** from **1.55MB** using the Windows XP resizing.

Receiving an Attachment

When the message (together with the attachment) is received into an **Inbox**, the presence of the 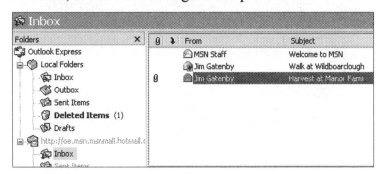 attachment is shown by a paperclip icon. This appears on the left of the entry for the message in the **Inbox**, as shown in the right-hand panel below.

Double-clicking the entry for the message in the right-hand panel of the **Inbox** opens up the message together with the attachment.

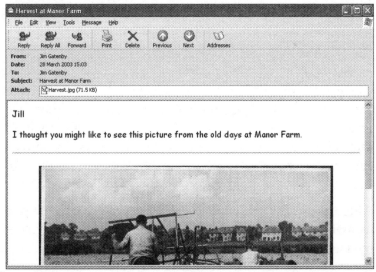

Double-click the entry in the **Attach:** field as shown on the right. The following dialogue box opens warning of the danger of viruses.

Subject:	Harvest at Manor Farm
Attach:	Harvest.jpg (71.5 KB)

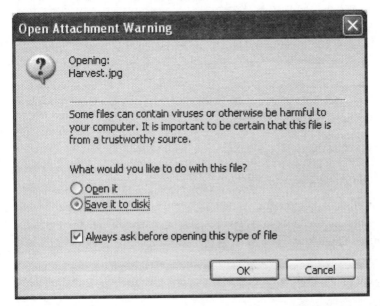

Open Attachment Warning

Opening:
Harvest.jpg

Some files can contain viruses or otherwise be harmful to your computer. It is important to be certain that this file is from a trustworthy source.

What would you like to do with this file?
○ Open it
⦿ Save it to disk

☑ Always ask before opening this type of file

OK   Cancel

Only select **Open it** shown above if you are absolutely sure of the source of the file. Otherwise select **Save it to disk**, in which case you will be asked to select a folder on your hard disc for the downloaded file. To be safe, any files you receive as e-mail attachments should be checked immediately, before opening them, using an up-to-date anti-virus program, like Norton AntiVirus or Dr. Solomon's Anti-Virus Toolkit.

After the file has been virus checked it can be opened up in its associated program (Word, Paint, Paint Shop Pro, etc.,) by double-clicking its name in the Windows Explorer.

Customising Your E-mails Using Stationery

The *Stationery* feature in Outlook Express can be used to make your outgoing e-mails more interesting. This involves creating a background which can fill part or all of the page. The background can be created from patterns and designs provided in Outlook Express. Or you can import a picture of your own and use it in the background. It is also possible to set a background colour and to select a font. Once you have created a design for your stationery it is saved along with several designs already provided in Outlook Express. Then you can select a stationery design to set the tone for a particular message you wish to send.

To create a new stationery design, select **Tools**, **Options...** and then click the **Compose** tab on the **Options** dialogue box, shown below. Under **Stationery** click **Mail** and then click the **Create New...** button.

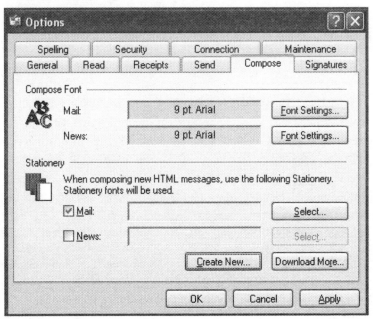

The **Welcome to the stationery wizard** window opens and on clicking **Next** the **Background** dialogue box opens as shown below.

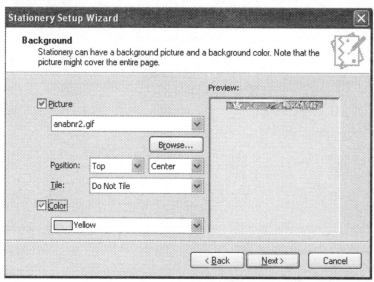

Click the box to place a tick next to **Picture** shown above. Click the down arrow just above the **Browse...** button to reveal a list of designs in **.gif** or **.jpg** format. Some of these designs only appear as a narrow strip across the top of the **Preview:** panel shown above. To use a graphic of your own click the **Browse...** button to select it from the folders on your hard disc.

You can change the **Position:** of the graphic using the drop-down menus currently showing **Top** and **Center** in the above screenshot. It is also possible to *tile* the graphic horizontally, vertically or to fill the whole page. A background colour for the entire page can be set by ticking the box next to **Color** and choosing from the drop-down menu, currently showing **Yellow** in the above screenshot.

On clicking **Next** you can set up your preferred style of text, using **Font:**, **Size:** and **Color:** as shown below.

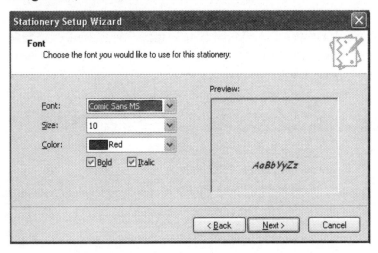

The next dialogue box allows you to set the left and top margins. Then you enter a name to save your stationery design before clicking **Finish** to complete the process.

To use this stationery when starting a new e-mail, click **Create Mail**, **Format** and **Apply Stationery**. Click **More Stationery** to display and select the new design you have created (**Milton** in this example) as shown below. Click **OK** to apply this stationery to the new e-mail message.

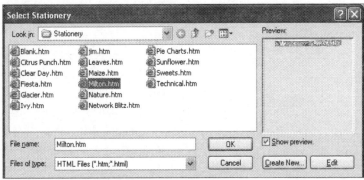

Adding a Signature to Your E-mail

Outlook Express allows you to add a few lines of text to all of your outgoing e-mails. This is known as a *signature*. Once it has been created, the signature is added automatically to a new e-mail. To create a new signature, from the main Outlook Express window select **Tools** and **Options....** Make sure the **Signatures** tab is selected.

You can type quite a lot of text in the **Edit Signature** box or alternatively import text from a **File**. Note the boxes at the top to include the signature on all outgoing messages other than **Replies** and **Forwards**. You can only have one signature per e-mail account. Click **Apply** and **OK** and the signature text will be added to all of the new e-mail messages you create.

E-mail Security

Outlook Express includes optional security features to ensure that e-mail can only be read by the intended recipients. Also to confirm that it really has been sent by the stated originator. There are two main parts of the security system in Outlook Express - *encryption* and the

digital ID. Once set up, these security features are launched from icons on the Toolbar in the **New Message** window of Outlook Express, shown left and below.

Encryption is a process of "scrambling" a message to make the text unintelligible to all but the intended recipients. The digital ID is an electronic method of proving your identity. It consists of the *digital signature* and two secret passwords, the *public key* and the *private key*.

Once set up you can use your digital ID to "sign" your outgoing e-mails to confirm your identity as the genuine sender; also to use encryption for the sending and receiving of private messages.

For someone to send you an encrypted e-mail, they must have your digital ID in their address book - which you can supply simply by sending then a digitally signed message. Your *public* key enables them to send you an encrypted message. Your *private* key enables you and you alone to read the message.

You can set up the security features in Outlook Express by selecting **Tools, Options...** and the **Security** tab. Then switch on (with a tick) the two check boxes under **Secure Mail** shown at the bottom of the **Options** dialogue box below. These turn on encryption and digital signing of outgoing messages.

To obtain your own **Digital ID** click the button shown above and on the right.

This connects to the Internet and opens up a Microsoft Web site displaying details of various *certifying authorities* or independent providers of digital IDs, such as VeriSign Inc. shown below. When you receive a digitally signed message, Outlook Express checks the security status of the digital ID with the certification authority.

Where to Get Your Digital ID

The following is a list of certifying authorities from which you can get a digital ID:

 VeriSign, Inc.

Verisign is Microsoft's preferred provider of digital IDs, and is the leading provider of digital authentication products and services. Through a special offer from VeriSign, Outlook users can obtain a free trial digital ID that you can use to positively identify yourself to, or receive encrypted messages from, business associates, friends, and online services when you use secure e-mail. VeriSign, Inc. and VeriSign's Certification Practice Statement.

Selecting one of these providers takes you to their Web site where you can look at their charges and, if you wish, set up your digital ID certificate.

 Digital ID Center

Secure Your E-mail

A VeriSign™ Digital ID™, or digital certificate, serves as an electronic substitute for a sealed envelope or your signature when you send messages across the Internet. Your Digital ID resides securely in your browser or e-mail software and allows you to digitally sign and encrypt your e-mail.

By digitally signing and encrypting your e-mail you can ensure that your confidential messages and attachments are protected from tampering, impersonation and eavesdropping.

 Class 1 Digital ID:

Act Now!
Only $14.95 for a
1yr personal ID

- . Authenticates your e-mail address
- . Automatic listing in our public directory and easy lookup of anyone else's Digital ID
- . US $1,000 of NetSure℠ protection against economic loss caused by corruption, loss, or misuse of your Digital ID
- . Free revocation and replacement if your Digital ID is lost or corrupted

US $14.95 per year

11

Working With Photographs

Introduction

In order to make good use of the Internet you need to be able to handle *digital photographs*. This might involve taking photographs with one of the new, inexpensive but effective *digital cameras* and transferring them to your computer's hard disc. Or it might mean using a *scanner* to copy old photographs from your family archive and saving them on your hard disc in digital form.

Once the photographs are stored on your hard disc they can be enhanced if necessary using one of several image editing programs such as Jasc Paint Shop Pro or Adobe Photoshop Elements. Such programs can be used, for example, to remove scratches from old photos, to remove "red-eye" or to change the contrast and brightness.

When you are happy with your photographs they can be e-mailed as *attachments* as discussed in Chapter 10 of this book. So in a few seconds your photographs might be delivered to friends and family, then printed out, anywhere in the world.

As discussed in the previous chapter, you may wish to display your photographs on your own pages on the Internet, so that anyone can view them.

The following basic equipment is needed to send and receive photographs using the Internet:

- A digital camera with a USB cable.
- A computer with an Internet connection.
- A spare *USB port* on the computer.
- A colour scanner.
- A colour printer.

Image editing software is also needed, such as Jasc Paint Shop Pro or Adobe Photoshop Elements. Windows XP can display photographs in different formats, as shown on the right. The Olympus digital camera package, described shortly, includes the Camedia CD with software for downloading, viewing, editing and printing photographs.

The Digital Camera

Until recently these were very expensive, but now there is a vast choice of digital cameras starting at around £40. While it is agreed that some of the cheaper digital models can't match the traditional 35mm for sheer quality, the digital camera has many advantages in terms of ease of use and convenience. For example, you can take a digital photograph, load it into your computer, edit it and print or e-mail it within minutes.

Shown below is the popular Olympus C-220 ZOOM digital camera costing about £200.

I have found this camera to be capable of taking perfectly acceptable pictures. An important feature of the digital camera is the *resolution*, i.e. the number of small *pixels* or *picture elements* which are the small squares used to make up an image. The Olympus C-220 Zoom has a resolution of 2 megapixels or 2 million pixels. Some models currently available use a resolution of 6 megapixels. The Olympus model has a zoom lens and a flash facility - not available on all digital cameras.

Memory

The main difference between the digital camera and the traditional 35mm camera is that the digital camera uses *memory* to store images, rather than film. The memory of a digital camera may be capable of holding over 100 images. The memory often takes the form of a plug-in card such as the  CompactFlash card and also the SmartMedia card shown on the right above. Whilst a camera may be supplied with an 8MB memory card as standard, a replacement 64MB card can currently be bought for under £20. It's a simple job to slide out the old card and replace it. Also available on some cameras are IBM Microdrives. These are miniature hard discs with a storage capacity of up to 1GB.

A new camera may be supplied with two standard AA batteries but it's advisable to replace these with nickel cadmium or nickel-metal hydride *rechargeable batteries*. Special kits are available which include a battery charger and four Ni-MH batteries. This enables you to have 2 spare batteries fully charged in reserve, useful when you are going on longer trips or on holiday.

On the back of the Olympus C-220 Zoom is a small LCD screen for taking and viewing photographs. This can also display a menu system for, amongst many other things, deleting photographs from the memory. The Olympus camera also has a facility for making short videos. These can be viewed on the small LCD at the back of the camera or by connecting the camera to a standard television with a special cable provided.

Transferring Digital Images to Your Computer

When you have taken a batch of photographs you can transfer them from the memory of your camera to your computer at any time. Your camera will probably come with its own software on a CD. To install this software simply place the CD in the CD drive of your computer. It should start up automatically and then it's just a case of following the instructions on the screen. In addition, if you are using a later version of Microsoft Windows such as Windows XP, there are a number of built-in features to assist with the handling and viewing of photographs.

Now fit the USB cable (which should have been provided with your camera) to the special socket in your camera.

Locate a spare USB port either at the back or the front of your computer. The USB ports are small rectangular sockets as shown below.

If you don't have a spare USB port then these can be obtained and fitted at any local computer store.

Devices which use the USB port not only work faster, but can be *hot swapped*, meaning that you can connect them while the computer is up and running.

On plugging the digital camera into the USB port on the computer, the following menu pops up on the screen.

Note on the above menu, there are options to print the photos directly, to view a slide show of the pictures in the **Windows Picture and Viewer**, to copy the photos into a folder on your hard disc and to open a folder to view the files. I normally save the photos on the hard disc - then they can be viewed, e-mailed or printed later.

On clicking **OK** a screen showing thumbnails of the images in your camera's memory appears. Then select with a tick the images to be copied to your hard disc.

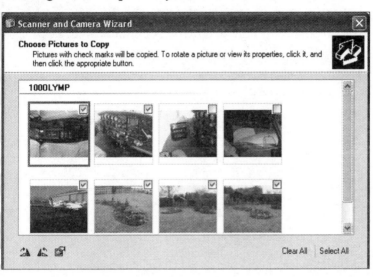

Next you can select the folder on the hard disc into which the photos are to be copied.

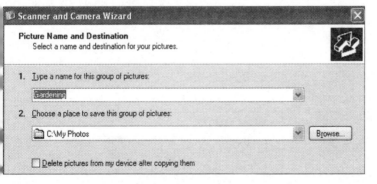

There is also an opportunity, after clicking **Browse...** above, to create your own new folder for the photographs.

The photographs are then copied to your chosen folder.

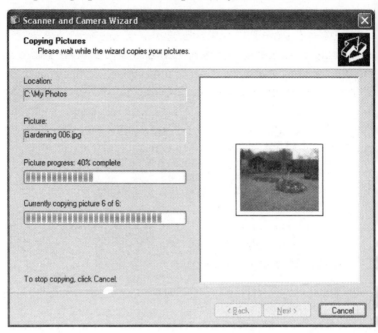

The photographs are stored on the hard disc in the **.jpg** format (sometimes also called **.jpeg**). This is the name of a file format (full name *Joint Photographic Experts Group*) especially suitable for storing photographs in a compressed form for sending as e-mails or for display in Web pages.

Scanning Old Photographs

Old photographs, even if they are quite tatty, can be scanned and stored on your computer. Once they are safely stored on your hard disc they can be enhanced in a digital image editing package like Paint Shop Pro or Adobe Photoshop Elements. Enhancing might include removing scratches or other damage which has occurred over the years. You might want to copy the photographs to CD for archiving the images in a more permanent form.

A4 Scanners can be bought for about £50 upwards and this includes the software to carry out a number of tasks. One of the popular Epson Perfection scanners is shown on the right.

Various scanning tasks can be carried out on photographs (and also other documents) up to A4 size and include:

- Copying and printing a photograph directly.
- Saving a photograph in a folder of your choice.
- Importing a photograph into another program.
- Sending a photograph to a Web site.
- Sending a photograph to be included with an e-mail message, as an attachment.

The scanner is started from the **All Programs** menu and the **Epson Smart Panel** is launched as shown below.

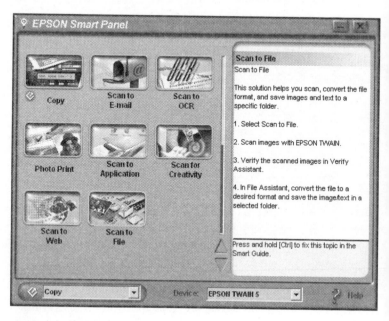

In this case I am scanning an image to be saved on the hard disc, so **Scan to File** is selected. Next a window opens showing the progress of the scan. The next window shows a thumbnail view of the document being scanned, with a default name. This can be altered to a name of your choice, as shown on the left.

On clicking **Finish** you can select **Browse** as shown below and then choose the folder in which to store the scanned image. In this case I have selected **C:\My Photos**. Then click the **Save** button shown below to place a copy of the scanned image on your hard disc.

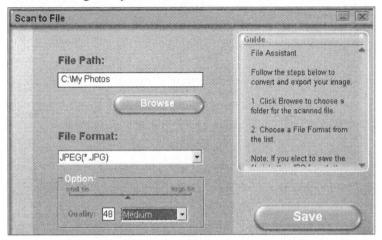

The **File Format:** shown above is most important for photographic work. This can be selected from the drop-down menu as shown below.

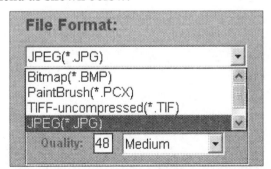

When saving photographs, the JPEG (*.JPG) format shown above is most suitable. This saves the photos in a very compact format without any obvious loss in quality.

The **Bitmap(*.BMP)** shown on the previous page is a common format used with Windows. This gives good quality but photographic files can be large - more than 20 times the size of a **.jpg** file for the same photograph.

In the above scanning operation, the same picture was scanned and saved twice, first in **.bmp** format and then in **.jpg** format. The two files are shown below in Explorer, with **View** and **Details** selected from the menu bar.

Name	Size
Jill David and Richard.bmp	4,572 KB
Jill David and Richard.jpg	154 KB

As shown above, the **.jpg** file is only about *one thirtieth* of the size of the **.bmp** file. When these two copies of the same photograph were printed out there was no obvious difference in quality. For this reason the **.jpg** is the most popular format for sending photographs as e-mail attachments, as shown in the last chapter. It is also very popular for photographs which are inserted in Web pages.

The **JPEG** file is often referred to as a "lossy" file. The file for the photograph is reduced in size by removing information which the human eye doesn't detect. So the **JPEG** file is very much smaller but with no appreciable loss in picture quality.

The reader may be confused by the use of both upper and lower case letters for the file types above. The form **.jpg** is often used when talking about an *extension to a file name* and **JPEG** (pronounced "jaypeg") is used to refer to the *name* of the file type.

Viewing Your Photographs

Windows XP can display photographs in a number of ways in the Windows Explorer. When you select **View** and **Details** off the menu bar, the display is as follows:

If you select **View** and **Thumbnails**, small editions of the photographs are displayed.

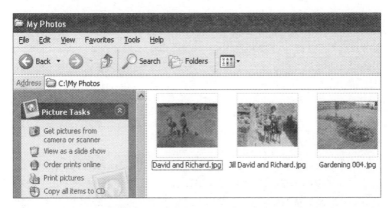

Notice on the left-hand side above, the **Picture Tasks** menu includes options to **Get pictures from a camera or scanner** and **View the pictures as a slide show**, where each photograph fills the whole screen. **Order prints online** connects you to the Internet, where you can e-mail your photographs to a company of your choice who will return glossy prints to your home address. **Print pictures** and **Copy all items to CD** are discussed shortly.

Another Explorer display format is obtained by selecting **View** and **Filmstrip**. This view allows you to scroll through the thumbnails and scrutinise them in the enlargement.

Double-clicking a photograph in any of the options off the **View** menu such as **Filmstrip**, **Thumbnail** or **List** opens up the **Windows Picture and Fax Viewer** shown below.

The **Windows Picture and Fax Viewer** shown on the previous page has several controls accessed by the icons along the bottom.

You can see the function of any of the icons by allowing the cursor to hover over the icon, causing an explanatory note to appear. The first two icons allow you to move backwards and forward through the photographs.

The next group of 3 icons allow the images to be resized to fit the viewer, to be displayed in actual size or to be viewed in a full-screen slide show.

Images can be viewed by zooming in and zooming out by clicking the usual magnifying glass icons shown on the right.

The next two icons allow the image to be rotated clockwise or anti-clockwise.

Images can be deleted by clicking the next icon shown as a cross, and this is followed by an icon to print the image on paper.

The next icon copies an image to another location such as a different folder or another disc or CD. The icon shown on the extreme right closes the **Windows Picture and Fax Viewer** and opens the image in a digital editing program such as Paint Shop Pro.

Editing Your Photographs

Photographs can be improved using a digital editing program. Some of the available software packages have an enormous range of features for capturing and enhancing photographs but the more basic features include:

- Importing pictures from a digital camera or scanner.

- Adjusting the brightness and contrast.

- Resizing, rotating and cropping the image.

- Removing unwanted defects such as scratches in old photographs or "red-eye" in portraits.

- Sending pictures to e-mail or posting on the Web.

If you have the Microsoft Office XP suite of programs, this includes **Microsoft Photo Editor**. This is launched from *start*, **All Programs** and **Microsoft Office Tools**.

Probably the best known image editing software is Adobe Photoshop, used by professionals and costing several hundred pounds. Paint Shop Pro is also very popular and powerful at under £100, together with Adobe Photoshop Elements and others for a similar price.

While Paint Shop Pro has an enormous range of features accessed from various menus, it is also very easy to use. The new user is helped by **Tutorials** and a **Product Tour** which demonstrates very clearly the main operations such as the removal of red-eye, for example, shown below.

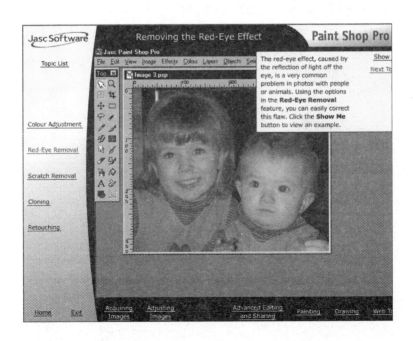

Archiving Your Photographs

You need to save photographs on your hard disc and then delete the images from the memory of the digital camera. This will free up the camera's memory, allowing you to take more photographs. However, for various reasons, items stored on your hard disc are not truly permanent.

For example, occasionally there are problems which require the hard disc to be wiped and then all the files and folders have to be reinstalled (assuming backup copies are available). Sometimes a folder may be deleted by accident. Photographs of friends or family are usually kept for many years, in which time you may change your computer several times. Therefore you need a permanent method of storing your photos which will stand the test of time.

Fortunately we have the ideal solution in the form of the *writeable CD*. These are virtually indestructible and can store hundreds of photos in the **.JPG** format. You also need a CD drive which can write or "burn" files to the CD. Many new PCs are fitted with *CD-Rewriter* drives, usually designated CD-RW. Otherwise you can buy a CD-RW drive for under £50 and it can be fitted in a few minutes.

Windows XP contains the necessary software to copy photos (and other sorts of files) to a CD. If you are using an earlier version of Windows, special CD burning software such as Ahead Nero and Easy CD/DVD Creator can be bought for around £40.

For storing photographs the *CD-R* disc is ideal. Although you can only write to these discs once, this limitation is not a problem when archiving photographs. A CD-R has a typical capacity of 700MB and when bought in packs of 25, say, can cost as little as 16 pence each.

Copying Photographs to CD Using Windows XP

Select the folder containing the photographs to be copied in the Windows Explorer a shown below.

In the **Picture Tasks** menu above select **Copy all items to CD**. (If the **Picture Tasks** menu is not visible, select **View** and **Explorer Bar** and make sure none of the options such as **History** and **Folders** are ticked). First the files are copied to a temporary folder. Then you are told you have **Files Ready to be Written to the CD**.

Now select **Write these files to CD** from the **CD Writing Tasks** menu shown on the bottom of the previous page. The **CD Writing Wizard** begins and you can enter a name for the CD. You are informed of progress as the writing proceeds.

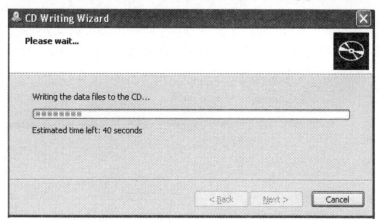

All being well, you will be informed that the CD writing process has been successful. Click **Finish** unless you want to click the box next to **Yes, write these files to another CD**.

Printing Your Photographs

The popularity of digital cameras has ensured there is a wide choice of colour printers capable of producing excellent photographic results. These are inkjet printers from firms such as Epson, Hewlett Packard, Canon and Lexmark. You will need to select **File**, **Print** and **Properties** to set the printer at its highest photographic print quality.

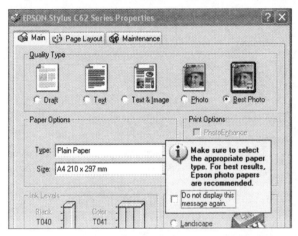

While these printers can be bought for as little as £50, the real cost is in the consumables. Black ink cartridges can cost around £20 and coloured ones nearly £30, for the genuine printer manufacturer's products. Cheaper versions are available from other suppliers at about a third of the price, although it has been claimed that these may damage the printer.

Printing on ordinary A4 printer paper obviously produces an inferior print quality to traditional photographic prints. For best results, special glossy photographic printer paper is available. This is quite expensive but produces excellent prints, comparable with conventional photographs.

Publishing Photographs on the Internet

You can post copies of your favourite photographs on the Internet for anyone in the world to view. With the folder containing your photographic files displayed in the Windows Explorer, make sure the **File and Folder Tasks** menu is displayed as shown below. If the **File and Folder Tasks** menu is not visible, select **View** and **Explorer Bar** and make sure none of the options such as **History** and **Folders** are ticked.

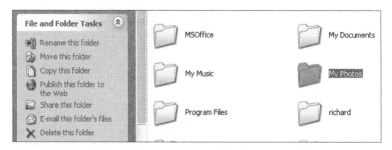

The wording on the **File and Folder Tasks** menu on the left above is altered depending on whether a **File** or a **Folder** is selected in the right-hand panel.

Note in the menu above there is an option to **E-mail this folder's files**. If you select this option the files will be prepared for sending as *e-mail attachments*. Your e-mail program will then be opened up ready for you to type an accompanying message. Sending photos and other files as e-mail attachments is covered in detail in the last chapter.

Now to copy our photographs to a Web site we select the **Publish this folder to the Web** option shown above. This starts the **Web Publishing Wizard** and after the initial **Welcome** screen, you can exclude any photos you don't want to publish by removing ticks from checkboxes on the icons for each picture, as shown on the next page.

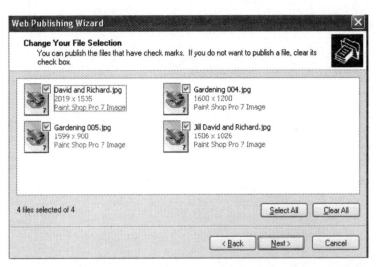

On clicking **Next**, the **Web Publishing Wizard** obtains information about your Internet Service Provider(s). After selecting your Internet Service Provider's Web location for storing the photographic files, you are given the opportunity to adjust the picture sizes before they are published on the Web.

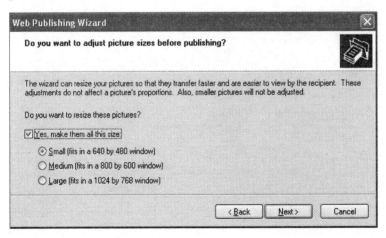

Then the process of copying the photo files to the Web begins and you are informed of progress, as shown below.

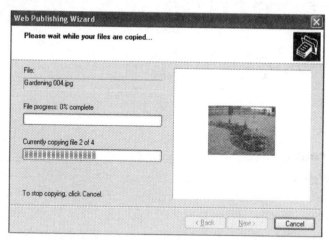

The Web Publishing Wizard should finish by telling you that you have successfully published your files. It should also give you the Web address where other people, such as friends and family around the world, can view your photographs by clicking on the file name as shown below.

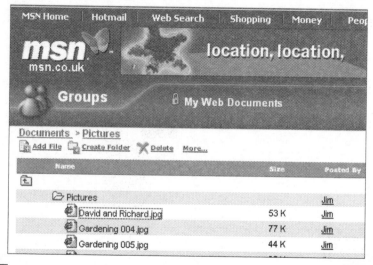

Creating a Simple Web Site

Introduction

A Web site consists of one or more pages of information stored on a special computer known as an Internet *server*, allowing access by millions of people. Web pages usually contain text and pictures but may also include other features such as links to other pages, buttons, menus, order forms, sound recordings, animations and video clips.

You can create your own Web site to post up information about a hobby, your business or your family. Then it can be viewed from anywhere in the world.

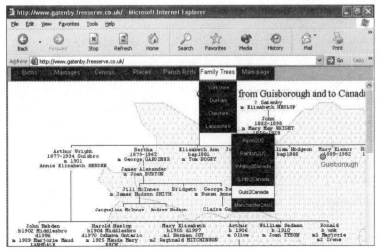

Space for Your Web Pages on an Internet Server

The Web server is a powerful computer located at the premises of an Internet Service Provider (ISP) - the company that provides your connection to the Internet, usually at the cost of a monthly subscription. Well known Internet Service Providers include AOL and The Microsoft Network.

The ISP should also allow you some space on one of its servers, on which to store your own Web pages. While you are developing your Web site, all of the new pages should be saved locally on the hard disc inside of your computer in your home or office, normally the **C**: drive. When the Web site is complete, all of the files can be *uploaded* and saved on the server of the company hosting your Web site, frequently the Internet Service Provider.

Web Browser

The Web browser is a program installed on all computers connected to the Internet, on which you can search the Internet and display Web pages. Two of the most well-known Web browsers are Microsoft Internet Explorer and Netscape Navigator.

Links

An important feature of all Web sites is the ability to move between pages by clicking on special underlined highlighted text, known as *hyperlinks*. These links enable the user to switch to different pages within the same Web site or to look at a completely

Return to Jim's Home Page

different Web site, perhaps on a server in another part of the world.

The Address of a Web Site: The Uniform Resource Locator

Each Web site has a unique address which enables a Web site to be found on the Internet. This address is known as the **Uniform Resource Locator (URL)**. To move to a particular site, the URL is entered into the **Address** bar of a Web browser, as shown below.

Web Page Content

Web sites are created by a diverse range of people for a variety of purposes. Someone might want to make information available to others who share a common interest such as a sport or a hobby. A large company or organization may use a Web site to promote its products and services or recruit staff world-wide.

A major advantage of using the World Wide Web to publish information is that facts and figures can be updated more quickly and easily than material printed by traditional methods in books and brochures. The Web can therefore be used to provide *up-to-date information* on national emergencies such as the 2001 epidemic of foot and mouth disease or the latest results of medical research. High quality information including graphs, maps, statistics and diagrams can be viewed on the screen or printed on paper.

Design Considerations

The actual Web pages are made up of instructions in a language known as HTML - HyperText Markup Language. This consists of lines of text laying out the page using words such as **center** and **color**. It's not particularly difficult to write Web pages using HTML but it can be a slow process. For this reason there are many software packages to do the job for you. Programs like Microsoft FrontPage and Macromedia DreamWeaver allow you to enter your text and graphics in a similar way to using a word processor. Then they save the Web page as a file in the HTML format.

Before starting work on producing a Web site, it's a good idea to sketch out a plan of each page, using pencil and paper. This will include the layout of text and pictures. If your site involves lots of individual pages connected by hyperlinks, then a plan showing the way they are to be linked will be useful.

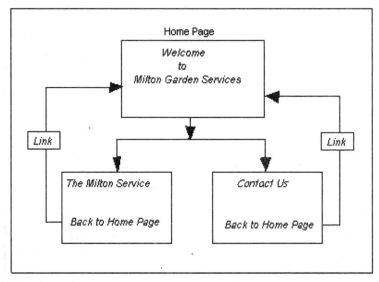

Looking at HTML

A page of HTML coding can look very complicated, but it's really just simple instructions to control the layout of the text and graphics on the Web page. In the example below a piece of text is centred and formatted as a large heading. **<h1>** is a *tag* which specifies the heading in a large font size.

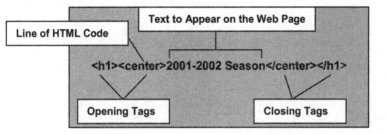

Viewing the HTML Code of Existing Pages

You can look at the HTML coding used to produce Web pages which are open in your browser. In Internet Explorer select **View** and **Source** from the menu bar as shown below for the Tarbert Hotel pages, discussed in Chapter 8.

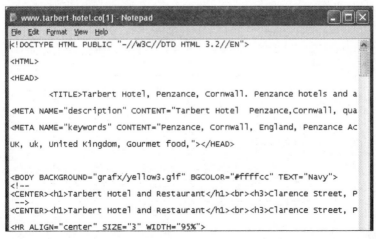

Methods of Creating HTML for Web Pages

There are various alternative ways to produce the HTML code for a Web page:

Using a Text Editor to Produce HTML Code

This method is relatively hard work and time consuming, since you have to learn the commands of the HTML language. You must also type all of the tags (such as **<h1>** and **<center>** shown on the previous page) as well as the page content itself. However, it's a cheap method since there's no need to buy expensive software and install it on your hard disc. A simple text editor like Microsoft Notepad is all you need and this is provided free with Microsoft Windows. If you understand HTML coding you will be able to tweak the coding produced by an HTML editor. This may be necessary to solve problems and achieve results which the dedicated Web design software cannot. The finished page is saved with the **.htm** or **.html** file name extension.

Using a Word Processor to Produce HTML Code

Using a word processor like Microsoft Word, or Lotus WordPro, simply enter and lay out the page as if it's a normal word processor document. Then select from the list of file types **Save as type: Web Page (*.htm: *.html)**, as shown below.

File name:	Creating a Web Site.doc
Save as type:	Word Document (*.doc)
	Word Document (*.doc)
	Web Page (*.htm; *.html)
	Web Page, Filtered (*.htm; *.html)
	Web Archive (*.mht; *.mhtml)

The word processing document is converted to HTML code by the software, so there's no need for you to know how to write the code. The word processor allows you to produce Web pages easily and cheaply, since most computers already have a word processing package installed. However, this method lacks many of the facilities of the special HTML editors discussed below.

Using an HTML Editor to Produce HTML Code

When using an HTML editor, i.e. Web page design program, you simply type out your Web pages as if using a word processor. Then the editor produces all of the HTML code for you. This includes the ability to insert powerful features such as colour, sound, music, animations and video clips, plus menus, buttons, links and tables. Ready-made *templates* allow professional-looking pages, rich in features and in a variety of styles, to be produced easily.

Well known HTML editors include Macromedia DreamWeaver, Adobe GoLive, Adobe PageMill and Microsoft FrontPage. Earlier versions of Internet Explorer include a free HTML editor called FrontPage Express and there is a more powerful version, Microsoft FrontPage. This program is included with some versions of Microsoft Office and can also be bought separately. For users of Microsoft Office, FrontPage has the advantage of a similar "look and feel" to programs like Microsoft Word, making FrontPage relatively easy to learn.

A Web design program saves a lot of work compared with typing HTML code. However, it's a good idea to have at least a little knowledge of HTML code to support your use of the HTML editor. If you enjoy a challenge you might wish to write your own HTML code - it's easy to learn and there are lots of books on the subject.

Creating a Simple Web Page Using FrontPage

It's quite easy to make a simple Web page - very similar to entering text into a word processor. For this exercise Microsoft FrontPage is used as it's powerful but not too expensive. The program is launched off the menu by selecting *start*, **All Programs** and **Microsoft FrontPage**.

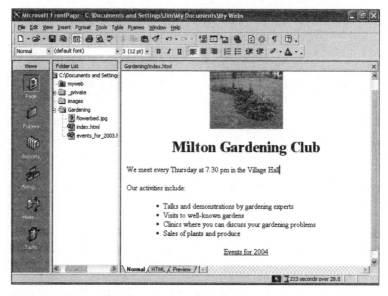

You can immediately start typing in text as you would in a word processor. The fonts and editing tools are available as icons on the Toolbar similar to those in Word, etc., including spelling, copy and cut and paste.

There is a full range of formatting tools on the right of the Toolbar, as shown below. Working from left to right, these include bold, italic and underline, together with justification, numbering, bullets and indentation.

Saving a Web Page

After you have typed in the text for a Web page it is saved using **File and Save As....**

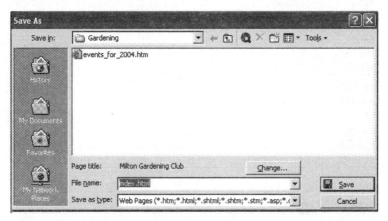

Notice above that it's normal for the **Home Page** of most Web sites to be saved with the name **index.htm**. This is the first page people will see when they connect to your Web site. Note also that Web pages are normally saved with the extensions **.htm** or **.html**, both being acceptable.

To save the Web page, enter the name **index.htm** and click **Save**. In the above **Save As** dialogue box, another Web page has already been created and saved with the name **events_for_2004.htm**. This page will be used shortly to show how a link is created.

Inserting a Picture into a Web Page

From the FrontPage Menu Bar, select **Insert**, **Picture** and **From File....** Then you can browse for the picture or photograph to be inserted.

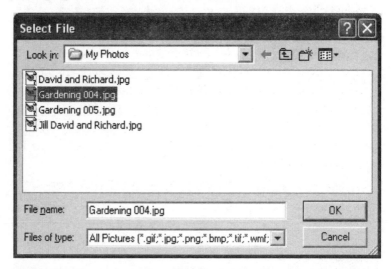

Click **OK** then once the picture is on the page it can be selected and resized by the 8 small squares or "grab-handles" around its perimeter. You can also move the picture to the left, right or centre using the icons shown on the right, normally used for formatting text.

As mentioned elsewhere in this book, photographs are normally stored in Web pages as **JPEG** files, having the **.jpg** extension to the file name, as shown above. This is a compact format producing small files which can be downloaded quickly from Web pages. Line drawings and Clip Art are usually saved as files with the **.gif** extension.

Creating a Link to Another Web Page

Using Microsoft FrontPage, you can create links (or *hyperlinks*) from one Web page to another. This may be on the same Web site or on a different Web site in another part of the world.

For this example I have already created and saved another Web page called **Events for 2004** as shown on page 203. On my main Web page, **index.htm** shown on page 202, I have typed the words **Events for 2004** and highlighted them. Now by clicking on the **Hyperlink** icon on the FrontPage Menu Bar, shown on the right, a link from the words **Events for 2004** is created, as shown in the **Create Hyperlink** window below.

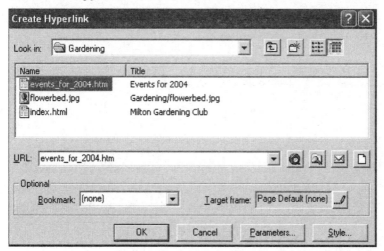

To create a link to the **Events for 2004** Web page, click its name and this will appear in the **URL:** box shown above.

Otherwise you can enter the address of the site you wish to link to, next to **http://** shown above.

Creating a New Folder for Your Web Files

It is convenient to keep all of the files for your Web site in one folder. This includes the **.htm/.html** files for the actual Web pages and any other files such as **.jpg** files for photos and **.gif** files for any drawings to be inserted. When you use the FrontPage editor to create a Web site, by default the files are automatically saved in the folder **...My Documents\My Webs** as shown below. This appears under the **Folder List** on the left of the FrontPage screen.

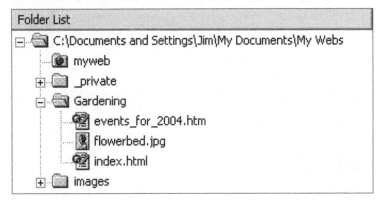

In the above example, I have created a new folder, **Gardening**, and saved in it the three files of my very simple Web site. These are the Home Page **index.html**, the second page **events_for_2004.htm** and the photo, **flowerbed.jpg**. (It doesn't matter above, that both **.htm** and **.html** were used. The file **events_for_2000.htm** was the name given by FrontPage, while I had entered **.html** in **index.html**.

Alternatively you can create a new folder for your Web pages by selecting **File** and **New** off the Menu Bar in the Windows Explorer. Then select this folder when using **File** and **Save As...** to save your Web pages in FrontPage.

The newly created folder can now be used for saving new Web pages. Any files needed for the new Web site which already exist in other folders can be moved into the new folder by dragging and dropping using the **Windows Explorer**.

Viewing and Testing Web Pages

After you have entered and saved a Web page it should be opened for checking in your Web browser, such as Internet Explorer. This can be done by using **File** and **Open** in Internet Explorer or by double-clicking the icon for the Web page in Windows Explorer, as shown below.

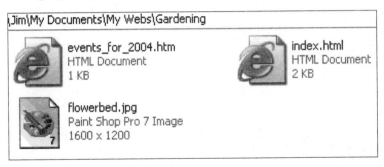

As you are likely to spend some time refining and developing the design before finally uploading it to the Internet, the browser should be set to work *off-line*, in order to avoid connection charges. Select **Work Offline** from the **Connect To** dialogue box, shown below, or **File** and **Work Offline** from the menu in Internet Explorer.

Apart from checking the details of the Web page, you may wish to improve the layout and the choice of text, etc. Links to other pages or Web sites should be tested. These can be corrected if necessary after returning to the text or HTML editor.

Editing Web Pages

When building a Web page it is often necessary to alternate between the HTML editor and the finished Web page in the browser, such as Internet Explorer. After viewing the finished page in the browser, you would return to the FrontPage editor to make any changes. To return to FrontPage from Internet Explorer, select **Edit with Microsoft FrontPage** as shown on the left below.

After the Web page has been edited it should be saved again with the **.htm** or **.html** extension and checked in Internet Explorer

To view the saved Web page in Internet Explorer after making any changes in FrontPage, select **File** and **Preview in Browser...**, as shown on the right above.

Publishing Your Web Pages

When you are happy with the pages you have created they should all be saved on the **C:** drive of your computer. All Web pages and associated pictures, photos or other files should be *saved in the same folder*.

Next the entire folder must be *uploaded* and saved on an Internet server computer. Then millions of people can (in theory) log on to the Internet and view your pages from anywhere in the world. When you subscribe to an Internet Service Provider, you may be allocated some free Web space (5-100MB perhaps) in which to save your work. Some Web hosting services might provide your own domain name e.g. **www.jimsmith.co.uk**, unlimited e-mail addresses and a counter to show how many people have visited your Web site.

If the purpose of a Web site will be to promote products or communicate information to as wide an audience as possible, the next important task is to attract people to your site. This is done by placing key words within the Web pages and registering your pages with the various *search engines* which people use to surf the Internet.

Uploading Your Pages to the Internet

You will need to obtain from your Internet Service Provider, the exact location on their server in which your Web site will be stored. From the **File** menu in FrontPage select **Publish Web...**. The following dialogue box appears.

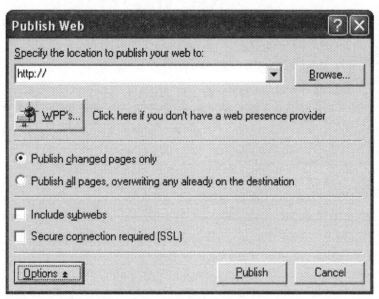

Enter in the location bar above, the precise address for your Web pages as provided by your Internet Service Provider. It may be something like: **ftp://ftp.myweb.mycompany.co.uk**

(**ftp** is a well established *File Transfer Protocol* and is used instead of HTTP shown above).

After you click **Publish** shown above, you will be asked to enter your user name and password. Then your Web pages will be uploaded to your own Web space and will then be accessible to the whole world. (The **Publish changed pages only** option shown above is used later to update your Web site with modified pages.)

More About
Modems

Why Is a Modem Needed?

The telephone network is the most common method of connecting a home or small business computer to the Internet. The telephone network was designed to transmit *sounds* and is known as an *analogue* system. However, inside the computer everything is represented as *binary digits*, a number system which uses only the digits *0* and *1*. There is an internationally agreed set of binary codes for each keyboard character, so that, for example, the letter *A* might be represented by *1000001* while a *space* might be *0100000*.

The purpose of a modem is to convert the binary digits *leaving* the computer into the analogue signals required by the telephone network. Similarly, analogue signals *entering* a computer from the telephone network are converted into digital data by the modem.

The term *binary digits* is usually abbreviated to the word *bits*. The speed of a modem for transmitting and receiving data is usually stated in *kilobits per second* or *Kbps*, as in the case of the *"56K"* modem. To be precise, in computing language, *K* actually means *1024*, rather than the usual *1000* in general use.

Internal and External Modems

The modem itself is a small set of microchips connected by cables between the computer and the telephone lines.

External modems are contained in their own box and sit outside of the computer on the desk. One cable connects the modem to the back of the computer. Another cable plugs into the standard telephone socket or "jack-plug". The external modem has an array of diagnostic lights which report on the current activities - such as whether the modem is switched on, or if it is sending or receiving data, fax or voice mail, etc. The external modem is portable - it can easily be unplugged and transferred to another computer. The external modem requires an extra power point and cables, unlike the internal modem.

The *Internal Modem*, shown below, consists of a small circuit board or *expansion card*, containing a set of chips.

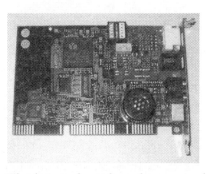

This plugs inside of the case of the computer. The internal modem obviously saves desk space and is more secure from damage or possible theft. The internal version takes its power off the computer itself.

The internal modem does not add to the bird's nest of wires at the back of the computer and does not need its own power point. Internal modems are generally cheaper than an equivalent external device.

56K Modem Versus Broadband

Initially broadband was too expensive for many ordinary users. Also, some telephone exchanges still need modification before they can handle the high-speed broadband service. However, at the time of writing, broadband is becoming increasingly popular as BT modifies more telephone exchanges. A number of companies such as BT, AOL, freeserve, Tiscali and Demon are promoting new broadband services.

The conventional 56K modem has a *nominal* data transmission rate of 56 kilobits per second (in practice often more like 33Kbps). ADSL broadband connections based on the BT telephone network are often claimed to be at least 10 times faster than 56K modems and some *cable modems* can exceed a rate of one *megabit* (approximately one million bits) per second. (To use *cable broadband* your street must be equipped for cable television).

Demanding applications such as the "streaming" (i.e. broadcasting) of video clips from the Internet require this extra speed. With the latest Internet connections, two or more computers connected across the Internet can share live voice and video links. So friends and families across the world can see moving pictures of each other while having a conversation.

Before long, therefore, the traditional 56K modem is likely to be superseded in many homes by the more powerful broadband systems. As discussed elsewhere in this book, some users only wanting to send and receive simple e-mails and indulge in limited surfing of the Internet may find it hard to justify the cost of broadband (currently about £25-£30 per month). Some 56K services are nominally "free" while others cost from £10 to £16 per month.

Overview - The Modem Installation Process

If you buy a new computer nowadays it will probably have a modem fitted as standard. If not you will need to have one fitted in order to connect to the Internet.

Alternatively you may already have an older machine with an unacceptably slow modem. (Not long ago modems of only 14.4 and 28.8Kbps were common). The old modem should be removed and replaced with a 56K model (or a broadband modem, if you can afford it). Aim to buy one of the later 56K models which comply with a standard known as V90 or V92. If you don't feel confident to do the work yourself, any good computer shop should be able to do the job in a few minutes.

However, it's not a difficult job to fit a modem. In the case of an external modem you don't even need a screwdriver. Simply place the modem on the desk and plug in a couple of cables and a power lead. Fitting an internal modem involves removing the computer casing and plugging the modem card into an available white PCI slot on the computer's main *motherboard*. Next restart the computer and the Windows operating system should detect the new modem, then install the necessary *driver* software. (Driver software is used to enable pieces of equipment from different manufacturers to work with the computer).

Safety Note - Static Electricity

To avoid possible damage to sensitive components, always rid yourself of static electricity before starting to "tinker" with the innards of a computer. This can be achieved by touching the frame of the computer, by touching water pipes or by wearing a special anti-static earthing strap, obtainable from electrical component stores.

The Control Panel

The Control Panel is an important software feature in Microsoft Windows and is used in the setting up and removal of hardware such as modems. As it will be referred to frequently throughout the next few pages, some essential features of the Control Panel are described here. There are several Control Panel *applets*, i.e. small programs represented by icons, which are used in this work and they are shown in the screenshot below. Start up the Control Panel from **start**, **Control Panel** and then click **Switch to Classic View** from the left-hand panel.

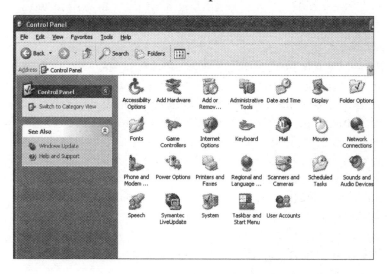

A number of icons shown above are relevant to the notes on modems which follow. These are **Phone and Modem...**, **System**, **Add Hardware** and **Network Connections**. To launch any of these features, double-click the appropriate icon. If you prefer to use the **Control Panel** in **Category View** then select **Switch to Category View** from the left-hand panel above.

Removing an Existing Modem

If you are replacing an old modem with a new one, you need to remove the *software* for the old modem before removing the modem itself. If you're fitting a new *external* modem, you can easily overlook the fact that an old *internal* modem is still hiding inside of the computer. The old modem could clash with the new one if both the hardware and the software are not completely removed.

The software for the old modem is removed using the **Device Manager**, launched by clicking *start*, **Control Panel** and double-clicking the **System** icon, as shown on page 215. Now select the **Hardware** tab and click the **Device Manager** button. Click the **+** next to **Modems** and *right-click* the name of your modem to reveal the menu shown below.

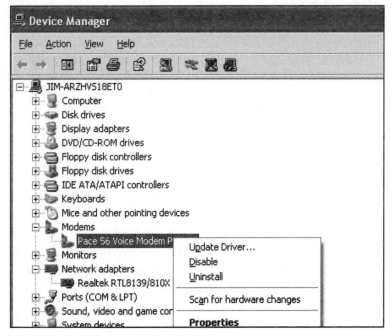

Click **Uninstall** as shown on the previous page and the software for the old modem will be removed. Another way to remove the modem software is to launch the **Control Panel** in **Classic View**, as described on page 215, and then double-click the **Phone and Modem Options** icon.

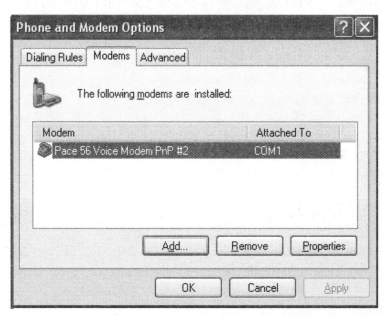

Highlight the name of the modem and click the **Remove** button shown above. Now shut down the computer and switch off the power. Rid yourself of static electricity as described on page 214. In the case of an external modem remove the old modem by simply undoing the cables.

In the case of an internal modem remove the case of the computer after undoing the small retaining screws. Undo the single retaining screw on the modem card and gently pull the old modem out of the PCI slot.

Fitting a New Modem

Make sure the computer is shut down and any previous modems have been uninstalled as just described. Divest yourself of static electricity as described on page 214.

Fitting an External Modem

Fitting an external modem is easy; you simply plug it into the outside of the computer without the need to remove the computer's metal casing. Most computers are provided with two *serial* or *communication* ports - designated as *COM1* and *COM2*. The ports have connectors at the back of the computer into which you plug the cables for peripheral devices like the mouse and an external modem. COM1 is often used to attach the mouse through a 9-pin connector. COM2 is located adjacent to COM1 and is frequently used for an external modem.

USB external modems, such as the new ADSL broadband modems, are also available. These plug into one of the small rectangular *USB* slots on the back of the computer. USB (or Universal Serial Bus) devices are designed to be easy to install and give ultra high speed performance.

Fitting an Internal Modem

The internal modem takes the form of an expansion card, as shown on page 212, which fits inside of the computer. To fit an internal modem you need a spare *PCI* slot inside of the computer. (PCI slots are white and shorter than the other slots). Remove the case of your computer. If necessary remove one of the blanking plates and carefully push the modem card into a vacant PCI slot. Make sure the card is fully engaged. Fit a retaining screw to the modem card and replace the case of the computer.

Detecting a New Modem

Later versions of Microsoft Windows, such as Windows XP, have been designed for *Plug and Play* installation of new hardware devices like modems. So when you restart your computer, Windows XP should detect the new modem, as shown by a small notice which appears at the bottom right of the

screen. (In the case of an external modem, make sure it is switched on first so that Windows can detect it on start-up.)

Installing the Modem Software

With true Plug and Play devices, Windows XP should find and install the necessary software from its own resources. This may not always be the case with a modem. If you open the **Control Panel** as described on page 215 and double-click the **Add Hardware** icon, you will start the **Add Hardware Wizard** as shown below.

On starting the **Add Hardware Wizard**, as shown on the previous page, if you have a hardware installation CD from your modem manufacturer, you are advised to click **Cancel**. Then insert the hardware CD, which should have been supplied with the new modem.

Although setup procedures vary for different products, the general principles are similar. The CD should start up automatically (a process known as "autobooting") on being placed in the drive. Then you may need to select the modem installation program from other options on the CD.

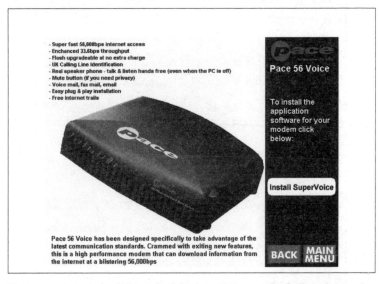

From now on it's simply a case of following the manufacturer's instructions on the screen. These often simply involve clicking **Next**, entering your name and other details and accepting or specifying a folder on your hard disc in which the modem software will be installed. You normally need to restart your computer to complete the installation of the modem software.

220

Examining the New Modem

There are several checks that you can do to ensure that the
new modem is correctly installed in your computer. Open
the **Control Panel** in **Classic Mode** as described on page
215. Now double-click the icon **Phone and Modem...** to
reveal the **Phone and Modem Options** window shown
below. Click the **Modems** tab.

As shown above, the **Generic SoftK56** modem has been
installed and attached to the **COM3** port. Right-click the
Properties button to obtain more information about the new
modem, as shown in the **Properties** window on page 223.

Another place to check for the presence of the new modem is in the **Device Manager**. From the **Control Panel**, double-click the **System** icon then select **Hardware** and **Device Manager**. You should see an entry for **Modems** which can be opened up by clicking the adjacent **+** sign.

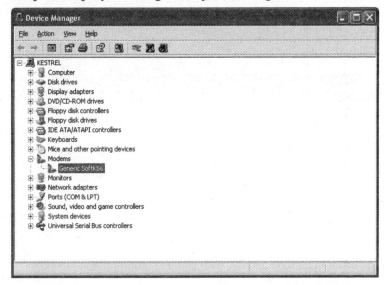

In this case the new modem, **Generic SoftK56** is listed. If your new modem does not appear as shown above or in the **Phone and Modem Options** window shown previously, you need to go through the installation procedure again. In the case of an internal modem, make sure the modem has been fully and evenly inserted into the PCI slot. (Care should be taken not to use excessive force). In some cases inserting the modem card into a different PCI slot may solve the problem. If an external modem is not listed in the **Device Manager** or **Phone and Modem Options** then check all cable connections and make sure there is power getting to the modem, indicated by a red light on the modem.

Restart the computer and check for the presence of the modem in the **Device Manager** or **Phone and Modem Options**.

A further check of a new modem is to look in the **Properties** window. This is opened by right-clicking over the modem's name in the **Device Manager** shown on the previous page. Then select **Properties** from the drop-down menu which appears.

The previous window is also accessible from the **Properties** button in the **Phone and Modems Options** window shown on page 221. Notice that the **Properties** dialogue box on the previous page contains the statement **This device is working properly** and there is also a button which starts the modem troubleshooter, if you are having problems.

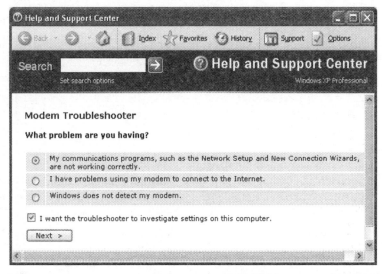

A further test is to select the **Diagnostics** tab from the **Properties** dialogue box and click the **Query Modem** button. If the word **Success** appears under **Response**, as shown below, then all should be well with the new modem.

Command	Response
ATQ0V1E0	Success
AT+GMM	COMMAND NOT SUPPORTED
AT+FCLASS=?	0,1,1.0
AT#CLS=?	0,1,8
AT+GCI?	COMMAND NOT SUPPORTED

Query Modem

Index

Further Reading

If you have enjoyed reading this book and found it helpful, you may also wish to read the companion volume, **Computing for the Older Generation,** illustrated below.

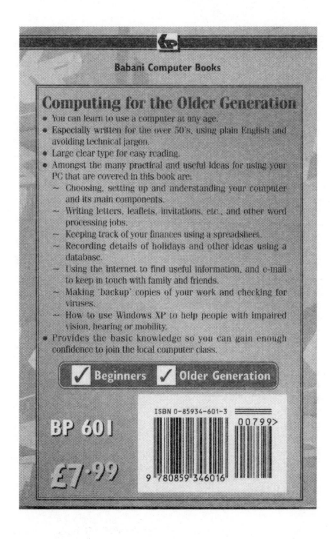